G000152051

SAMS
Teach Your

MICROSOFT®
WORD 2000

Peter Aitken

in 10 Minutes

SAMS

A Division of Macmillan Computer Publishing
201 West 103rd St., Indianapolis, Indiana, 46290 USA

SAMS TEACH YOURSELF MICROSOFT WORD 2000 IN 10 MINUTES

Copyright© 1999 by Sams Publishing

International Standard Book Number: 0-672-31441-X

Library of Congress Catalog Card Number: 98-86986

Printed in the United States of America

First Printing: April 1999

01   00   99   4   3   2   1

TRADEMARKS

WARNING AND DISCLAIMER

EXECUTIVE EDITOR
Jim Minatel

DEVELOPMENT EDITOR
Jill Hayden

ACQUISTIONS EDITOR
Renee Wilmeth

TECHNICAL EDITORS
Nick Goetz
Paul Leininger
Don Roche

MANAGING EDITOR
Thomas F. Hayes

COPY EDITOR
JoAnna Kremer

INDEXER
Tonya Heard

PROOFREADER
Jeanne Clark

INTERIOR DESIGN
Aren Howell

COVER DESIGN
Gary Adair

LAYOUT TECHNICIANS
Cynthia Davis-Hubler
Brad Lenser

CONTENTS

About the Author

Peter Aitken is a widely read computer book author, with more than two dozen books to his credit, including *10 Minute Guide to Lotus 1-2-3*. He lives in Chapel Hill, North Carolina, and is employed at Duke University Medical Center.

Acknowledgments

While this book has but a single author, it is in many ways a team effort. Renee Wilmeth, Acquisitions Editor, and Jill Hayden, Development Editor, were instrumental in converting my rough chapters into a finished product. Don Roche, Technical Editor, made sure that no technical errors slipped through. Thanks, everyone.

TELL US WHAT YOU THINK!

As the reader of this book, *you* are our most important critic and commentator. We value your opinion and want to know what we're doing right, what we could do better, what areas you'd like to see us publish in, and any other words of wisdom you're willing to pass our way.

As the Executive Editor for the General Desktop team at Sams Publishing, I welcome your comments. You can fax, email, or write me directly to let me know what you did or didn't like about this book—as well as what we can do to make our books stronger.

Please note that I cannot help you with technical problems related to the topic of this book, and that due to the high volume of mail I receive, I might not be able to reply to every message.

When you write, please be sure to include this book's title and author as well as your name and phone or fax number. I will carefully review your comments and share them with the author and editors who worked on the book.

Fax: 317-581-4770

Email: `office_sams@mcp.com`

Mail: Executive Editor
General Desktop Applications
Sams Publishing
201 West 103rd Street
Indianapolis, IN 46290 USA

INTRODUCTION

Welcome to Microsoft Word 2000. The latest release of Microsoft's flag-
ship word processing program brings even more power and features to a
program that was already considered to be the best of its type. No matter
what kind of document you need to create—a simple memo, a World
Wide Web page, or a 500-page report—Word can handle it, and make you
look good in the process!

Word is surprisingly easy to use, but any program with so much power
cannot avoid being somewhat complex. How do you go about learning the
ins and outs of Word so that you can start using it to get something done?
You can go to a bookstore and buy one of those 1,200-page books that
covers every single part of Word in excruciating detail—but do you have
time to read a 1,200-page book? What you need is a quick way to learn
the important parts of Word, those parts of the program that you'll need
most often in your day-to-day word processing tasks. Let me say mod-
estly that you have chosen exactly the right book!

The *Sams Teach Yourself in 10 Minutes* is designed for people just like
you. In these pages, you learn the basics of Word in a series of short,
easy-to-understand lessons. Each lesson is self-contained and can be com-
pleted in 10 minutes or less, permitting you to start and stop as your
schedule allows. There's no padding in this book—it's loaded with clear,
concise information that you can really use.

WHAT IS THE *SAMS TEACH YOURSELF IN 10 MINUTES*?

The *Sams Teach Yourself in 10 Minutes* series takes a different approach
to teaching people how to use a computer program. We do not attempt to
cover every detail of the program. Instead, each book concentrates on the
program features that are essential for most users, the features that you
need to get your work done. Our goal is to teach you, as quickly and pain-
lessly as possible, those things that you need to start using the program
for productive, real-world work.

USING THIS BOOK

Sams Teach Yourself Microsoft Word 2000 in 10 Minutes contains 27 lessons. Ideally, you will work through them in order. After reading the first five lessons, however, you can skip around to find specific information as quickly as possible. When you complete the book, you will have a good knowledge of the most important parts of Word, and you will be capable of completing almost all word processing tasks with ease.

Several special elements are used throughout the book to highlight specific types of information:

Timesaver Tip   Helpful suggestions to get you working more efficiently.

Plain English   Non-technical definitions of terms that might be unfamiliar to some readers.

Panic Button   Warning of possible problems, and information on how to solve them.

Several of the book's other features are designed to make your learning faster and easier:

- Numbered steps provide exact instructions for commonly needed procedures.

- Menu commands, toolbar buttons, and dialog box options that you select, and text that you enter, are printed in **boldface and blue** for easy recognition.

- Messages that appear onscreen are **boldface**.

LESSON 1

GETTING STARTED WITH MICROSOFT WORD

In this lesson, you learn how to start and exit Word and to identify the parts of the Word screen. You also learn the basics of entering text.

STARTING WORD FOR WINDOWS

Start Word from the Windows Start menu, following these steps:

1. Open the Start menu by clicking the **Start** button.

2. On the Start menu, click **Programs**.

3. On the next menu, click **Microsoft Word**.

Another way to start Word is to open the Start menu and click **New Office Document**. Or, if the Office Shortcut Bar is displayed along the right edge of your screen, click the **New Office Document** button. Either way, the New dialog box appears. In this dialog box, select the **General** tab (if necessary), and then double-click the **Blank Document** icon.

 Can't Find Microsoft Word? Some installations of Word differ as to where items are placed on the Start menu. If you cannot find Microsoft Word or New Office Document in the specified locations, look at other parts of the Start menu. If you can't find Microsoft Word on the Start menu, please refer to the product documentation for installation instructions. You must properly install Word (or Office) on your system before you can use it.

UNDERSTANDING THE WORD SCREEN

When you start Word, you see a blank document. Before you begin to enter text, however, you need to know about the various parts of the screen (see Figure 1.1). You'll use these screen elements, which are described in Table 1.1, as you work on your documents.

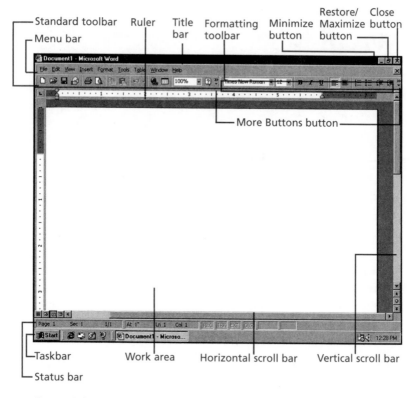

FIGURE 1.1   When you start Word, a blank document appears on your screen.

TABLE 1.1   PARTS OF THE WORD SCREEN

SCREEN ELEMENT	FUNCTION
Work area	Your document displays here for text entry and editing. Figure 1.1 shows a blank document.
Ruler	Above the work area, the ruler indicates in white the document area that is within your margins. The ruler also indicates any indents or manually placed tab stops.
Title bar	The program name and the name of the current document display here. At the right end of the title bar are buttons to minimize, restore, and close the program.
Menu bar	Menu headings on this bar enable you to access Word's menu commands.
Standard and Formatting toolbars	The small pictures, or buttons, on the toolbars enable you to select commonly used commands by clicking the mouse.
Status bar	Word displays information about the document and the state of the keyboard lock keys on the status bar.
Scroll bars	You click on the scroll bars to move around in your document.
Minimize button	Click this button to temporarily hide Word. Then, click the Microsoft Word button on the taskbar at the bottom of your screen to re-display Word.
Close button	Click this button to close Word.
Restore/Maximize button	Click this button to enlarge Word to full-screen or to shrink Word to a partial-screen window.

ACCESSING COMMANDS THROUGH MENUS AND TOOLBARS

As you use Word, you issue commands to tell Word what you want done. You can carry out most Word commands using either the menus or the toolbars. The method you use depends on your personal preference.

To select a menu command,

1. Open a menu by clicking the menu title on the menu bar. You can also open a menu by holding down the **Alt** key, and then pressing the underlined letter in the menu title. For example, press **Alt+F** (hold down **Alt** and press **F**) to open the File menu.

2. A short menu is displayed with those commands that are needed most often, plus any commands you have used frequently. You can select a command at this point by double-clicking the menu command (as explained in step 3), or you can display the full menu by clicking the down arrow at the bottom of the menu. Even if you do nothing, the full menu displays automatically after a few seconds.

3. On the open menu, click the desired command or press the underlined letter of the command name.

Throughout this book, I use a shorthand to specify menu commands; for example, if I say click **File, Open,** it means to open the **File** menu, and then select the **Open** command.

 Change Your Mind? If you change your mind about a menu command, you can either press the Esc key twice or click anywhere outside the menu to close the menu without making a selection.

Figure 1.2 shows the open File menu. There are several elements used by Word menus to provide you with additional information. Table 1.2 explains these elements.

Button   Ellipsis

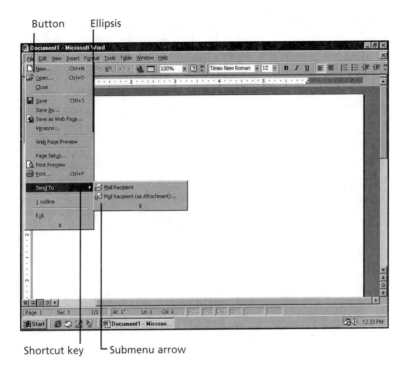

Shortcut key   └ Submenu arrow

Figure 1.2 Displaying the File menu enables you to access the Send To submenu.

TABLE 1.2 PARTS OF A MENU

MENU ELEMENT	FUNCTION
Button	If the menu command has a corresponding toolbar button, a small picture of the button is displayed to the left of the menu command.
Ellipsis (…)	Indicates that the menu command leads to a dialog box.
Submenu arrow	Indicates that the menu command leads to another menu (called a submenu).
Shortcut key	Identifies the keys you can use to select the menu command using the keyboard.

You can use shortcut keys to select some commands without using the menus at all. Shortcut keys are listed on the menu next to the corresponding command. In Figure 1.2, for example, you can see that the shortcut key for the Open command is **Ctrl+O**. This means that pressing **Ctrl+O** (press and hold the **Ctrl** key, press the **O** key, then release both keys) has the same effect as clicking **File, Open**.

To use the toolbars, simply use your mouse to click on the desired button. The buttons have pictures on them to help you identify each button's function. You can jog your memory by resting the mouse cursor on a button for a few seconds without clicking. Word displays a ToolTip next to the button, identifying the button's function.

Word normally displays both the Standard toolbar and the Formatting toolbar in the same row, just below the menus (as shown in Figure 1.1). Depending on the size of your display screen, Word might not be capable of displaying all the toolbar buttons at the same time. When this happens Word displays a More Buttons button at the right end of each toolbar. Click on this button to display the remaining buttons, then click on the desired button. Buttons that you use in this way are added to the visible part of the toolbar.

 What's This? Press Shift+F1 to activate What's This help (the mouse pointer displays as an arrow with a question mark). Click on any element on the Word screen to view information about that element.

CHANGING THE WAY MENUS DISPLAY

You can tell Word to always display the full menus, without a delay and without requiring you to click on the arrow at the bottom of the menu. To turn off adaptive menus:

1. Click **Tools, Customize** to display the Customize dialog box.

2. In the dialog box click the **Options** tab.

3. Click the **Menus Show Recently Used Commands First** check box to remove the checkmark next to it.

4. Click the **Close** button.

Figure 1.3 shows how the File menu and Send To submenu display with adaptive menus turned off. Compare this with Figure 1.2, which has adaptive menus turned on.

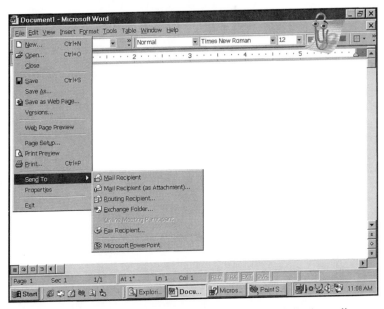

FIGURE **1.3**   With adaptive menus turned off, Word displays all items under the menu without delay.

The remainder of this book assumes that adaptive menus are turned off.

WORKING IN DIALOG BOXES

Many of Word's commands result in the display of a dialog box. Word uses dialog boxes to obtain additional information required to carry out a command. Each dialog box is different, but they all use the same basic elements.

In a dialog box, press the **Tab** key to move from item to item; press **Shift+Tab** to move backward. You can click an item or press **Alt** plus the underlined letter to select an item. When the dialog box selections are complete, press **Enter** or click the **OK** button to accept your entries and carry out the command. To close the dialog box without carrying out the command, click the **Cancel** button or press **Esc**.

ENTERING TEXT AND MOVING AROUND

Word displays a blinking vertical line in the work area. This is the cursor or insertion point, and it identifies the location in the document where text will be inserted and where certain editing actions will occur. To enter text, simply type it on the keyboard. Do not press **Enter** at the end of a line— Word automatically wraps the text to a new line when you reach the right margin. Press **Enter** only when you want to start a new paragraph.

If you make a mistake, there are a couple of ways to delete it:

- Press the **Backspace** key to erase characters to the left of the cursor.

- Press the **Delete** key to erase characters to the right of the cursor.

  Undo That Edit!   You can use Word's **Undo** command to recover if you make a mistake or change your mind: select **Edit**, **Undo** or press **Ctrl+Z**. The Undo button is also found on the Standard toolbar and can be used to undo a string of commands, starting with your last.

You can move the cursor around to add and edit text in different document locations. Table 1.3 describes the basic cursor movements.

TABLE 1.3   MOVING THE CURSOR

TO MOVE THE CURSOR...	DO THIS
To any location in the text	Click the location with the mouse
One character right or left	Press the left or right arrow key
One line up or down	Press the up or down arrow key
To the start or end of the line	Press the **Home** or **End** key
To the start or end of the document	Hold the **Ctrl** key and press **Home** or **End**

You'll learn more about moving around Word in Lesson 3, "Basic Editing Tasks."

QUITTING THE PROGRAM

When you are finished working with Word, you have several options for exiting the program, all of which have the same result:

- Click **File, Exit.**
- Press **Alt+F4**.
- Click the **Close** button on the title bar.

If you have an unsaved document, Word prompts you to save it before exiting. For now, you can just select **No**. You'll learn about saving documents in Lesson 4, "Saving and Opening Documents."

In this lesson, you learned how to start and exit Word and how to use menus and toolbars, and you learned about the basics of entering and editing text. The next lesson, "Creating a New Document," shows you how to create a new Word document.

LESSON 2

CREATING A NEW DOCUMENT

In this lesson, you learn how to create a new Word document and about the relationship between documents and templates. You also learn how to save time with wizards.

UNDERSTANDING DOCUMENT TEMPLATES

To work effectively with Word, you must understand that every Word document is based on a *template*. A template is a model for a document. Even a brand new document you open with the New Document button is based on the Normal template.

Some templates contain no text, giving you a blank document with some basic formatting specifications in which you are responsible for entering all the text. The Normal template is of this kind. Other templates contain text and detailed formatting specifications; for example, if you write a large number of business letters, you might use a template that contains the date, your return address, and a closing salutation. When you create a new document based on that template, all those elements are automatically included in the document—all you need to do is add the other parts. If a template contains formatting, then all documents based on that template have a uniform appearance (the same font and margins, for instance).

Word comes with a variety of predefined templates that are ready for you to use. These templates cover a range of common document needs, such as fax forms, memos, business letters, and Web pages. You can also create your own templates. In this lesson, you learn how to use Word's predefined templates. Lesson 24, "Creating and Modifying Document Templates," shows you how to create your own.

 Document Template A model for a new document that can contain text and formatting.

STARTING A NEW BLANK DOCUMENT

Many of the documents you create are based on the Normal template, which creates a blank document. As you learned in Lesson 1, "Getting Started with Microsoft Word," when you start Word it automatically opens a blank document for you to work with. If Word is already running, you can create a new blank document by clicking the **New Blank Document** button on the toolbar.

To start a document based on another template, follow these steps:

1. Click **File**, **New**. The New dialog box appears (see Figure 2.1).

2. The tabs along the top of the dialog box list the different template categories. Click the tab corresponding to the type of document you want to create.

3. Click the icon that corresponds to the template you want. If a preview of the template's appearance is available, it appears in the Preview area. Figure 2.1 shows a preview of the Contemporary Letter template.

4. Click **OK**. Word creates the document and displays it, ready for editing.

When you create a document based on a template, the template's text and formatting are displayed in the new document. There is nothing special about document text that comes from a template—you can edit it just like any other text. You can also edit the actual templates, as you'll learn in Lesson 24.

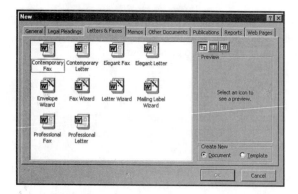

FIGURE 2.1   Select a template for your document in the New dialog box.

Word on the Web: Web Templates   Select the **Web Pages** tab in the New dialog box for templates that are useful for Web documents.

Some templates contain placeholder text that you must replace. For example, the Contemporary Letter template contains a dummy company name and other items that you must delete and replace with your own information. For example, the document says "[Click here and type your name]." Some items are displayed in brackets, whereas others are not. Simply follow the instructions that are displayed in the template.

No Templates?   If you can't find any templates, they probably were not installed with Word. You can rerun the Word Setup program and choose the **Add or Remove Features** option to install additional templates. Some templates are listed in the New dialog box but are not actually installed until the first time you use them. You need your Word or Office CD-ROM to do this.

SAVING TIME WITH WIZARDS

Some of Word's templates are a special kind of template called a *wizard*. A wizard is an active tool that asks you questions about the document you want to create and uses your answers to invent the new document, whereas a standard template is a static combination of text and formatting. When you're starting a new document, you can recognize a wizard in the New dialog box by its title and by the small magic wand in its icon. You can see several wizard template icons in Figure 2.1. Each wizard is unique, but they all follow the same basic procedures. There are a number of steps in a wizard, each of which asks you for certain information about the document you want to create. Figure 2.2 shows an example (a step in the Letter Wizard), and Table 2.1 describes the different components of the wizard dialog box.

TABLE 2.1   PARTS OF A WIZARD DIALOG BOX

WIZARD COMPONENT	FUNCTION
Title bar	Shows the name of the wizard that is running, and the step you are on.
Step tabs	Graphically represents the wizard steps, with the current step highlighted. Click any step to go directly to that step.
Information area	Requests document information from you.
Cancel button	Cancels the wizard without creating a new document.
Back button	Moves to the previous wizard step.
Next button	Moves to the next wizard step.
Finish button	Ends the wizard and creates the new document based on the information you have entered so far.
Help button	Click to display Help information about using the wizard.

Title bar   Information area   Step tabs

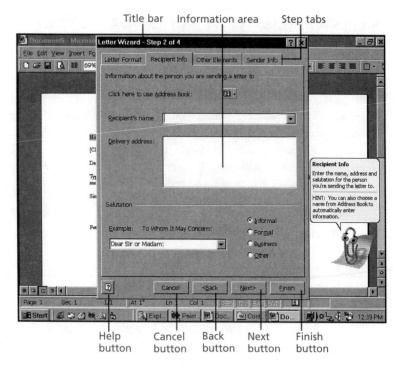

Help   Cancel   Back   Next   Finish
button   button   button   button   button

FIGURE 2.2   The Letter Wizard walks you through the steps to creating a letter.

To create a new document using a wizard, follow these steps:

1. Click **File, New** to open the New dialog box (refer to Figure 2.1).

2. Click the tab corresponding to the category of document you are creating. (Not all tabs contain wizards.)

3. Click the icon of the wizard you want to use, then select **OK**. At this point, several of the wizards bring up the Office Assistant with a question. After you answer the question, you go on to complete the wizard. To hide the Office Assistant for the remainder of the wizard, right-click on it and choose **Hide**. For more about the Office Assistant, see Lesson 5, "Using the Help System."

4. In the wizard dialog box, enter the necessary information—based on how you want the document created—then click **Next**.

5. Repeat step 4 for each of the wizard steps. If needed, click **Back** or use the step buttons on the flow diagram to return to an earlier step to make changes in the information.

6. At the last wizard step, click **Finish** to close the wizard and create the new document.

 Know Your Templates   Spend some time becoming familiar with Word's various predefined templates—they can save you a lot of time.

In this lesson, you learned about document templates and how to create a new document. You also learned how to use wizards. The next lesson, "Basic Editing Tasks," teaches you how to perform basic editing tasks in Word.

Lesson 3

Basic Editing Tasks

In this lesson you learn how to enter text, move around in a document, and perform other basic editing tasks.

Entering Text

When you start a new Word document based on the Normal template, you see a blank work area that contains only two items:

- **Blinking vertical line**   This is the *cursor*, or *insertion point*; the cursor marks the location where the text you type appears in the document, and where certain editing actions occur.

- **Horizontal line**   This marks the end of the document.

In a new, empty document these two markers are at the same location. To enter text, simply type it using the keyboard. As you type, the text appears and the insertion point moves to the right. If the line of text reaches the right edge of the screen, Word automatically starts a new line; this is called *word wrapping*. Do not press **Enter** unless you want to start a new paragraph. As you enter more lines than will fit on the screen, Word scrolls previously entered text upward to keep the cursor in view. Figure 3.1 illustrates word wrap, the end of document marker, and the cursor.

 Leave It to Word Wrap   Press Enter only when you want to start a new paragraph.

Press Enter to start a new paragraph

Press Enter to skip a line

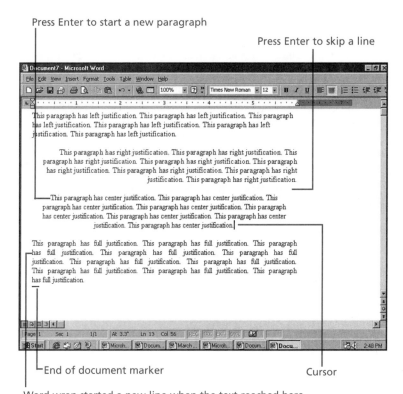

End of document marker   Cursor

Word wrap started a new line when the text reached here

FIGURE 3.1 Use Enter only to start a new paragraph.

DEFINING PARAGRAPHS IN WORD

Defining paragraphs is important in Word because certain types of formatting only apply to individual paragraphs. In Word, you end one paragraph and start a new one by pressing **Enter**. Word inserts a new, blank line and positions the cursor at the beginning of it.

 Entering Blank Lines To leave a blank line between paragraphs, press **Enter** twice at the end of the first paragraph.

On your screen, the result might look the same as if word wrap had started the new line, but the difference is that Word has inserted a paragraph mark. These marks are normally invisible, but you can display them by clicking the **Show/Hide ¶** button on the Standard toolbar. Click the button again to hide the marks. This tool is very useful when you need to see exactly where the paragraphs begin and end in your document, and to distinguish word-wrap line breaks from paragraphs.

 What Are All Those Other Marks? When you display paragraph marks, Word also displays spaces as dots and tabs as arrows.

What happens if you enter text in two paragraphs and then decide you want it all in one paragraph? To combine two paragraphs into a single paragraph, follow these steps (you can do this with or without paragraph marks displayed):

1. Move the cursor to the beginning of the first line of the second paragraph.

2. Press the **Backspace** key to delete the paragraph mark. The second paragraph moves up to join—and assume the formatting of—the first paragraph.

MOVING AROUND THE DOCUMENT

As you work on a document, you often have to move the cursor to view or work on other parts of the text. Most of the time you'll use the mouse (as explained in Table 3.1). If the desired cursor location is in view on the screen, simply click on the location. If the desired location is not in view, you must scroll to bring it into view, and then click on the location.

TABLE 3.1   SCROLLING WITH THE MOUSE

TO SCROLL...	DO THIS
Up or down one line	Click the up or down arrow on the vertical scroll bar.

To Scroll...	Do This
Up or down one screen	Click the vertical scroll bar between the box and the up or down arrow.
Up or down any amount	Drag the scroll bar box up or down. The scroll bar box indicates what page you are on as you drag it up or down the scroll bar.
Up or down one page	Click the **Previous Page** or **Next Page** button on the vertical scroll bar.

 Click to Move the Cursor Note that scrolling with the mouse does not move the cursor; the cursor remains in its original location and the screen displays another part of the document. You must click the new location to move the cursor.

Table 3.2 explains how to move around in the document using the keyboard.

TABLE 3.2 MOVING THE CURSOR WITH THE KEYBOARD

To Move...	Perform This Action
Left or right one character	Press ← or →
Left or right one word	Press **Ctrl+←** or **Ctrl+→**
Up or down one line	Press ↑ or ↓
Up or down one paragraph	Press **Ctrl+↑** or **Ctrl+↓**
To the start or end of a line	Press **Home** or **End**
Up or down one screen	Press **Page Up** or **Page Down**
To the top or bottom of the current screen	Press **Ctrl+Page Up** or **Ctrl+Page Down**
To the start or end of the document	Press **Ctrl+Home** or **Ctrl+End**

Quick Go To   Press Shift+F5 one or more times to move the cursor to the locations in the document that you edited most recently.

SELECTING TEXT

Many tasks that you perform in Word require that you first select the text that you want to modify. For example, to underline a sentence you must select the sentence first and then click the **Underline** button. Selected text appears on the screen in reverse colors, as shown in Figure 3.2 (which has the phrase "Thank you for considering me for the vacant" selected).

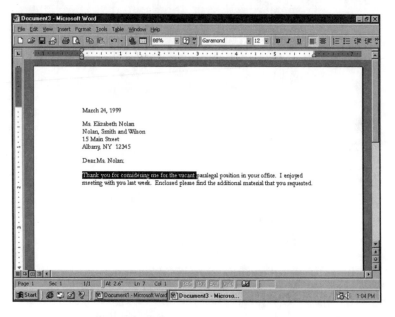

FIGURE **3.2**   Selected text appears in reverse colors.

You can select text with either the mouse or the keyboard. With the mouse, you can use the selection bar, an unmarked column in the left document margin. When the mouse pointer moves from the document to the selection bar, it changes from an I-beam to an arrow pointing up and to the right. Table 3.3 lists the methods you can use to select text.

TABLE 3.3   METHODS OF SELECTING TEXT

To Select Text	Perform This Action
With the Mouse	
Any amount	Move the mouse until the I-beam is at the start of the text, press and hold the left mouse button, and drag the highlight over the text.
One word	Double-click anywhere on the word.
One sentence	Press and hold **Ctrl** and click anywhere in the sentence.
One line	Click the selection bar next to the line.
Multiple lines	Drag in the selection bar next to the lines.
One paragraph	Double-click the selection bar next to the paragraph, or triple-click anywhere in the paragraph.
Any amount	Click at the beginning of the text, press and hold **Shift**, and then click at the end of the text.
Entire document	Press and hold **Ctrl** and click anywhere in the selection bar.
With the Keyboard	
Any amount	Move the insertion point to the start of the text, press and hold **Shift**, and move the insertion point to the end of the desired text using the movement keys described in Table 3.1.
Entire document	Press **Ctrl+A**.

To cancel a selection, click anywhere on the screen or use the keyboard to move the insertion point.

When you are selecting text by dragging with the mouse, Word's default is to automatically select entire words. If you need to select partial words, you can turn this option off (or back on) as follows:

1. Click **Tools, Options** to open the Options dialog box.

2. Click the **Edit** tab.

3. Click the check box for **When Selecting, Automatically Select Entire Word** to turn it on or off.

4. Click **OK**.

DELETING, COPYING, AND MOVING TEXT

In Lesson 1, "Getting Started with Microsoft Word," you learned how to use the **Delete** and **Backspace** keys to delete single characters. In this lesson, you learn how to delete larger amounts of text in a single block, and how to move or copy text from one document location to another.

To delete a block of text, first select the text, and then choose from the following:

- To simply delete the text, press **Delete** or **Backspace**.

- To delete the text and replace it with new text, type the new text.

To move or copy text, start by selecting the text, and then follow these steps:

1. To copy the text, click **Edit, Copy** or press **Ctrl+C**.

   Or, to move the text, click **Edit, Cut** or press **Ctrl+X**.

2. Move the cursor to the location where you want to place the moved or copied text.

3. Click **Edit, Paste** or press **Ctrl+V**.

Use the Toolbar to Cut and Copy You can use the Cut, Copy, and Paste buttons on the Standard toolbar when moving or copying text.

You can also use the mouse to copy or cut, and then drag and drop text. This technique is most convenient for small amounts of text, and when the "from" and "to" locations are both visible onscreen. Follow these steps:

1. Select the text.

2. Point at the text with the mouse. The mouse pointer changes from an I-beam to an arrow.

3. To copy the text, press and hold **Ctrl**. To move the text, do not press any key.

4. Drag to the new location. As you drag, a vertical dotted line indicates the text's new location.

5. Release the mouse button and, if you are copying, the **Ctrl** key.

 Make a Mistake? You can recover from most editing actions, such as deleting text, by clicking **Edit, Undo** or by pressing **Ctrl+Z**.

When you cut or copy text, Word places it on the Clipboard. Then, when you paste, you get the most recent text that you cut or copied. Windows 98 Clipboard can hold as many as 12 items, and you can use the multiple-item feature as follows:

1. Cut (or copy) some text to the Clipboard as previously described, and then immediately cut or copy another section of text. Word displays the Clipboard dialog box, as shown in Figure 3.3.

Paste All button

Copy button ———

Icons ———

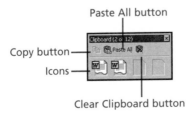

Clear Clipboard button

FIGURE **3.3** The Clipboard dialog box can contain up to 12 items.

2. Items in the Clipboard are represented by icons, and empty slots are represented by blank icons. With this dialog box displayed, you can do the following:

   - View the contents of a Clipboard item by resting the mouse pointer over the icon for a moment.

   - Paste an item's text into the document by clicking the icon.

   - Paste the entire Clipboard contents into the document by clicking the **Paste All** button. Items are pasted in the order they were cut or copied.

   - Copy text from the document to the Clipboard as a new icon by selecting the text in the document, and then clicking the **Copy** button.

   - Delete the entire Clipboard contents by clicking the **Clear Clipboard** button.

3. When you are finished, click the **Close** button to close the dialog box.

In this lesson, you learned how to enter text, move around the document, and perform other basic editing tasks. You also learned how to copy and move text. In the next lesson, "Saving and Opening Documents," you'll learn how to save and retrieve documents.

LESSON 4

SAVING AND OPENING DOCUMENTS

In this lesson, you learn how to name your document, save it to disk, and enter summary information. You also learn how to open a saved document.

SAVING A NEW DOCUMENT

When you create a new document in Word, it is stored temporarily in your computer's memory under the default name Document*n*, where *n* is a number that increases by one for each new unnamed document. The document is only kept in memory until you quit the program or turn off the computer. To save a document permanently so that you can retrieve it later, you must assign a name and save it to a disk or drive:

1. Click **File**, **Save**, or press **Ctrl+S**. The Save As dialog box appears (see Figure 4.1).

2. In the **File Name** text box, enter the name you want to assign to the document file. The name can be up to 256 characters long and needs to be descriptive of the document contents.

3. If you want to save the document in a different folder or drive, do one of the following:

   - Click the **Save In** drop-down arrow and select a different folder and/or drive.

   - Select one of the folder icons displayed at the left side of the dialog box.

   - If the folder is visible in the dialog box list, double-click it.

4. Click **Save**. The document is saved to disk and the name you assigned appears in the title bar.

Folder icons   Save In box

Dialog box list

Figure 4.1   Use the Save As dialog box to save a document for the first time.

  Word on the Web   Documents you make publicly available on your Web site must be in *hypertext markup language* (*HTML*) format. There is a separate command for saving in this format: click **File**, then **Save as Web Page**.

Saving a Document as You Work

After naming and saving a document, you still need to save it periodically as you work to minimize data loss in the event of a power failure or other system problem. After you name a document, there are several ways in which you can easily save the current version:

- Click **File, Save**.

- Click the **Save** button on the Standard toolbar.

- Press **Ctrl+S**.

Word automatically uses the document's current name to save it, and no dialog boxes appear. The previous version of the file is overwritten.

Don't Forget! Save your document regularly as you work on it, or you might lose your work in the event of a power outage or other problem.

Save All Documents If you are editing more than one document (as covered in Lesson 23, "Working with Multiple Documents simultaneously"), you can save them all at once by holding **Shift** when you click the **File** menu, and then clicking **Save All** on the menu.

SAVING A DOCUMENT UNDER A DIFFERENT NAME

After you name a document, you might need to change its name. For example, you can keep an old version of a document under its original name and save a revised version under a new name. To change a document name, follow these steps:

1. Click **File, Save As**. The Save As dialog box appears, and shows the current document name in the File Name text box.

2. In the File Name text box, change the filename to the new name.

3. (Optional) Select a different folder in the **Save In** list box to save the document in a different folder. Click the **Create New Folder** button to create a new folder in which to save the document.

4. Click **Save**. Word saves the document under the new name.

Staying Organized with Document Properties

Every Word document has a set of properties that provide information about the document, such as the name of the person who created it, the date it was created, and the date it was last edited. Some properties contain summary information that you enter, whereas others contain information that is automatically generated by Word. This information can be useful when you are trying to locate a specific document or to use a document created by someone else.

To enter or view a document's properties, follow these steps:

1. Click **File, Properties** to open the Properties dialog box.

2. Click the **Summary** tab, as shown in Figure 4.2.

3. Enter or edit summary information as described in the following list.

4. Click **OK**. Document properties are saved along with the document.

A document's properties are saved with it, but do not display or print as part of the document.

Following are the summary information properties you will use most often:

- **Title**   Enter the title of the document. This is a descriptive title that you assign and is not the same as the document's filename.

- **Subject** Enter a phrase that describes the subject of the document.

- **Author** Word automatically fills this field with the username you entered when you installed the program. You can change it if necessary.

- **Company** Your company name. This might be automatically entered for you based on your Windows installation.

- **Category** Enter a word or phrase that describes the type of document.

- **Keywords** Enter one or more words related to the document contents.

- **Comments** Enter any additional information you want saved with the document.

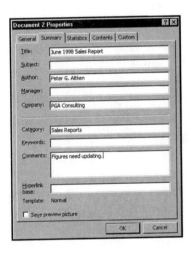

FIGURE 4.2 Enter summary information in the Document Properties dialog box.

Word automatically generates useful statistics about each document, such
as the number of words it contains and the date and time the document
was created. To view a document's statistics, click **File, Properties**, and
then click the **Statistics** tab.

> **Quick Word Count** To get a quick count of the words
> and other elements in your document, click **Tools**,
> then **Word Count**. To count words in a specific part
> of the document, select the text and then click **Tools**,
> then **Word Count**.

OPENING A SAVED DOCUMENT

You can open any document created with Word for Windows to continue
working on it. You can also open documents that were created with other
programs, such as WordPerfect.

To do so, click **File, Open**, or press **Ctrl+O**. The Open dialog box
appears, as shown in Figure 4.3.

> Quickly display the Open dialog box by clicking the
> Open button on the Standard toolbar.

The main list in this dialog box shows all the Word documents and folders
in the current folder. Both Word documents and Web pages are identified
by a small page icon next to their name; the Word document icon has a
"W" on a blank page whereas the Web page icon has a "w" on a page
with a globe on it. Folders display a file folder icon. The Look In list box
shows the name of the current folder. You can take the following actions
in the Open dialog box:

- To open a file, click its name in the file list and choose **Open**.

- To preview the contents of a document or its properties, click the
  filename, then click the down arrow next to the Views button and
  select either **Properties** or **Preview**.

- To look for files other than Word documents, click the **Files of Type** drop-down arrow and select the desired document type.

- To move up one folder in the hierarchy, click the **Up One Level** button.

- To move down one level to a different folder, double-click the folder name in the file list.

- To move to another folder, click the **Look In** drop-down arrow and select the desired folder, or click the folder icon on the left side of the dialog box.

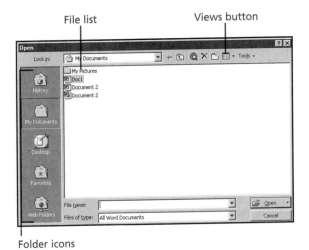

Folder icons

FIGURE 4.3 Use the Open dialog box to open a document for editing.

To quickly open a document you recently worked on, you can use Word's Recently Used File List rather than the Open dialog box. To view this list, click **File** to open the **File** menu. The list is displayed at the bottom of the menu just above the **Exit** command. To open a file on the list, press the number corresponding to the file or click the filename with the mouse.

This list displays the document files that you have saved most recently. If you have just installed Word, there are no files displayed here, of course. If you have saved files and the list still doesn't display, see the next paragraph.

You can control how many files appear on the Recently Used File List, and whether the list appears at all:

1. Click **Tools, Options** to open the Options dialog box. Click the **General** tab if necessary.

2. Click the **Recently Used File List** check box to turn it on or off.

3. To change the number of files displayed in the list, enter a number in the **Entries** text box, or click the up/down arrows to change the existing entry.

4. Click **OK** when you're finished.

 Quick Open You can open a Word document (and start Word if it is not already running) by double-clicking the document name or icon in the Windows Explorer or My Computer window.

In this lesson, you learned how to name your document, save it to disk, and enter summary information. You also learned how to open a document that you saved earlier. The next lesson, "Using the Help System," shows you how to use Word's online Help system.

LESSON 5

USING THE HELP SYSTEM

In this lesson you learn how to use Word's online Help system and the Office Assistant.

DIFFERENT KINDS OF HELP

Word has several methods by which you can obtain help. They can be divided into three categories:

- **The Office Assistant** Offers advice about what you are doing and answers questions you ask.

- **The Help Topics window** Provides a Table of Contents, Index, and search facility for the online Help information.

- **What's This Help** Enables you to get information about any item on the screen simply by clicking it.

ASKING THE OFFICE ASSISTANT

You have probably already met the Office Assistant; it's the animated character that pops up to give you advice. The *Office Assistant* is a very powerful Help system that keeps track of what you are doing and makes intelligent guesses about what information you need. There are several different assistant "characters" available, so don't worry if yours is different from the one shown in the figures.

By default, the Office Assistant is displayed and sits on top of whatever you're working on. You can hide the Office Assistant by clicking **Help**, then **Hide the Office Assistant**. To show the Assistant again, click **Help**, then **Show the Office Assistant**.

Where's My Office Assistant Command? If the Office Assistant command is not available on the Help menu, it means the Assistant has not been installed. You must run the Word setup program again, selecting the **Add or Remove Features** option to install the Office Assistant.

THE KINDS OF HELP OFFICE ASSISTANT PROVIDES

The Office Assistant offers help in two ways. One way is automatic—as you work, it keeps track of what you are doing and displays help information for certain tasks. For example, if the Office Assistant is displayed and you start a numbered list by typing the numbers yourself, the Assistant recognizes what you are doing, converts the text to Word's automatic numbered list format (which is covered in detail in Lesson 12, "Creating Numbered and Bulleted Lists"), and displays a help balloon as shown in Figure 5.1.

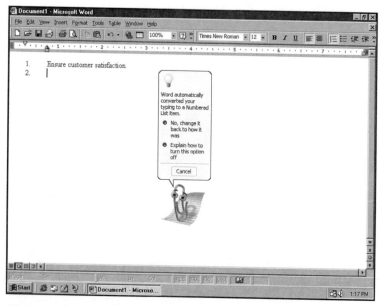

Figure 5.1 The Office Assistant displays information related to the task you are performing, such as creating a numbered list.

When the help balloon is displayed, you can select one of the bulleted help items by clicking it, or you can hide the balloon and return to your document by clicking **Cancel**.

The Office Assistant can also respond to specific questions that you ask. Use the following steps to ask a question:

1. Click on the Office Assistant to open the help balloon, as shown in Figure 5.2. If you've used the Assistant previously, the balloon will contain help information from your last request.

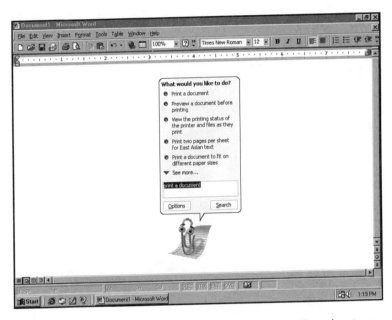

Figure 5.2   You can ask the Office Assistant a question about using Word.

2. Type in a question, such as "How do I print a document?" You can also type in a word or phrase of interest such as *line spacing* or *spelling*. Then press **Enter** or click **Search**.

3. The Assistant displays a list of related help topics. Click on the specific topic of interest to view detailed information. If there are more topics than can fit in the balloon, click **See More** at the bottom of the list to view the additional items.

CUSTOMIZING THE OFFICE ASSISTANT

You can customize the appearance of the Office Assistant and determine
how it operates.

1. Click the Office Assistant.

2. Click the **Options** button to display the Office Assistant dialog
   box (shown in Figure 5.3).

3. On the Options tab, select options to control how the Office
   Assistant works.

4. On the Gallery tab, select the desired appearance of the Office
   Assistant.

5. Click **OK**.

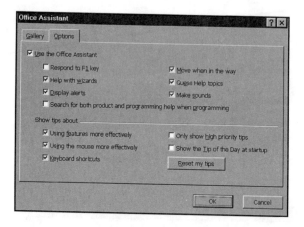

Figure 5.3   You specify the appearance and operation of the
Office Assistant in the Office Assistant dialog box.

USING THE MICROSOFT WORD HELP WINDOW

When you select a specific topic from the Office Assistant balloon, or if
you are not using the Office Assistant and press **F1**, the Microsoft Word
Help window is displayed. Normally, this window is displayed on part of

the screen so that your document remains visible; however, you can expand it to the full screen (as shown in Figure 5.4) by clicking the **Maximize** button at the right end of the title bar.

The Help window is comprised of the following parts:

- **Information Panel**   Displays help information on the current topic.

- **Buttons**   Enable you to perform various actions (explained as follows).

- **Tabs**   Provide access to different parts of the Help system.

In the Information panel, you can view information related to the current help topic. You can also take the following actions in this panel:

- Click an underlined term or phrase to view information on that topic.

- Click a highlighted term or icon to view a pop-up window with information about the term or icon.

- Click a **Show Me** icon to have Help walk you through the steps to carry out a specific task.

While viewing Help information you can use the Help window buttons to perform the following actions:

- To hide the tabs and display the Information panel at maximum size, click the **Hide** button. Click this button again to redisplay the tabs.

- To move back in the list of viewed help topics, click the **Back** button.

- To move forward in the list of viewed help topics, click the **Forward** button.

- To print the current help topic, click the **Print** button.

- To select Help options, click the **Options** button.

Information panel   Buttons

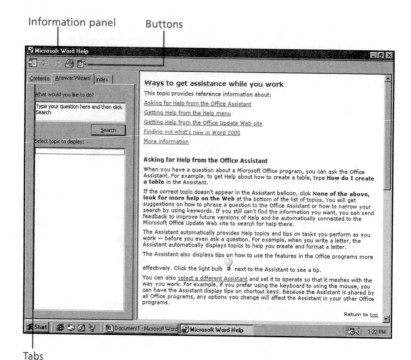

Tabs

Figure 5.4 You can find help information in the Microsoft Word Help window.

 Customizing Your Help Window   You can change the relative sizes of the Information Pane and the tabs area of the Help window by pointing at the vertical border between them, and then dragging it to the desired position. You can also resize the entire Help window, or you can maximize or minimize it (like any other screen window).

USING THE ANSWER WIZARD TAB

In the Help window's Answer Wizard tab (shown in Figure 5.4), you can ask a question, just as you do with the Office Assistant. To ask a question, do the following:

1. Type your question, or a phrase of interest, in the What Would You Like To box.

2. Click the **Search** button or press **Enter**. Word displays a list of related topics in the Select a Topic to Display box.

3. Click the specific topic to display related information.

USING THE CONTENTS TAB

The Contents tab, shown in Figure 5.5, organizes the Help information by subject and in a hierarchical fashion. At the top level is a series of books, each identified by a book icon next to the title. Each book can contain additional books as well as topics which in turn contain the Help information. A topic is identified by an icon of a page with a question mark on it.

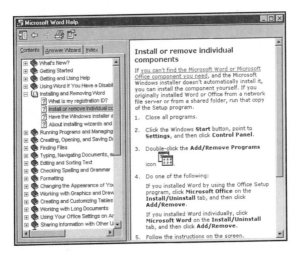

Figure 5.5   You can locate Help information using the Contents tab.

On the Contents tab, you can perform the following actions:

- To open a book and display its contents, click the adjacent **plus** (+) sign or double-click the book's title. An open book has an open book icon next to it.

- To close a book and hide its contents, click the adjacent **minus** (–) sign or double-click the book's title.

- To open a topic, click its title.

USING THE INDEX TAB

The Index tab in the Help Topics window provides another way to access Help information. As shown in Figure 5.6, the Index presents you with an alphabetical list of the available Help keywords. To locate a topic by keyword, use the following steps:

1. Select a keyword in the Or Choose Keywords list by clicking it. Or, you can start typing a keyword in the Type Keywords box and the list automatically scrolls to the first matching entry.

2. When the desired keyword is selected, click the **Search** button. Word displays a list of matching topics in the Choose a Topic box.

3. Click a topic to display its information.

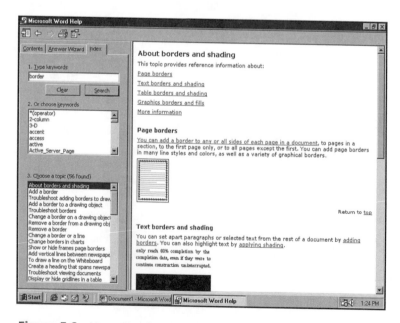

Figure 5.6   You can select Help keywords on the Index tab.

USING WHAT'S THIS HELP

Word's What's This Help feature gives you Help information about items that are visible onscreen. There are two ways to activate What's This Help:

- When a dialog box is open, click the **question mark (?)** button in the title bar.

- When a dialog box is not open, press **Shift+F1** or click **Help, What's This.**

Either way, the mouse cursor changes to an arrow and a question mark. Click the screen item of interest to display a pop-up window with information about the selected item.

 Word on the Web   If you have an Internet connection, you can click **Help, Office on the Web,** and then select the desired subject to be connected to Microsoft's related Web site.

In this lesson, you learned how to use Word's Help system. The next lesson, "Finding and Replacing Text," shows you how to find and replace text in your document.

LESSON 6

FINDING AND REPLACING TEXT

In this lesson, you learn how to find specific text in your document and how to automatically replace it with new text.

SEARCHING FOR TEXT

Word can search through your document to find occurrences of specific text. Word's default is to search the entire document, unless you select some text before you issue the command.

If you want the search limited to part of the document, select the text first (otherwise Word will search the entire document); then, follow these steps:

1. Click **Edit**, **Find**, or press **Ctrl+F**. The Find tab of the Find and Replace dialog box appears (see Figure 6.1).

2. In the Find What text box, enter the text you want to search for. The text you enter is called the search template.

3. Click **Find Next**. Word looks through the document for text that matches the search template. If it finds matching text, it highlights it in the document and stops—with the Find and Replace dialog box still displayed.

4. Click **Find Next** to continue the search for another instance of the template. To close the dialog box and return to the document, press **Esc** or click **Cancel**. The found text remains selected.

When you have searched the entire document, or if the search template cannot be found, a message is displayed informing you of the search status.

 Repeat Searches When you open the Find and Replace dialog box, the template for the last successful search is still displayed in the Find What text box. This makes it easy to repeat the previous search.

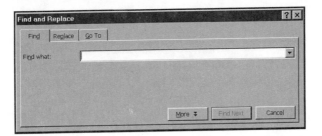

Figure 6.1 To locate text in your document, use the Find and Replace dialog box.

 Search Template The search template is the model for the text you want to find.

USING SEARCH OPTIONS

The default Find operation locates the search template you specify without regard to the case of letters or whether it's a whole word or part of a word. For example, the template *the* finds *the*, *THE*, *mother*, and so on. You can refine your search by using Word's search options. To do so, click the **More** button in the Find and Replace dialog box. The dialog box expands to offer additional options (see Figure 6.2).

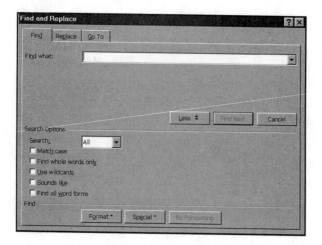

Figure 6.2 You can fine-tune your search by setting options for the Find command.

You can choose from the following options:

- **Match Case** Requires an exact match for upper- and lowercase letters. By selecting this check box, *The* matches only *The* and not *the* or *THE*. This option can be used in conjunction with the Find Whole Words Only option.

- **Find Whole Words Only** This matches whole words only. By selecting this check box, *the* matches only *the*—not *mother*, *these*, and so on. This option can be used in conjunction with the Match Case option.

- **Use Wildcards** Permits use of the * and ? wildcards in the search template. The * wildcard matches any sequence of zero or more characters, whereas the ? wildcard matches any single character. The template *th?n* matches *thin*, *then*, but not *thrown* or *thn*. The template *th*n* matches *thin*, *thn*, *thrown*, and so on.

- **Sounds Like** Finds words that sound similar to the template. By selecting this check box, for example, *their* matches *there*.

- **Find All Word Forms**   Locates alternative forms of the search template. For example, *sit* matches not only *sit* but also *sat* and *sitting*. This check box is not available if you select the **Use Wildcards** check box.

To control the extent of the search, click the **Search** drop-down arrow and select one of the following options:

- **All**   Searches the entire document.

- **Down**   Searches from the cursor to the end of the document.

- **Up**   Searches from the cursor to the beginning of the document.

Can't Find It?   If you can't find text that you're sure is in the document, check the spelling of the search template and make sure unwanted search options are not enabled.

FINDING AND REPLACING TEXT

Word's Replace command enables you to search for instances of text and replace them with new text. To replace text, click **Edit**, **Replace**, or press **Ctrl+H**. The Replace tab of the Find and Replace dialog box appears (see Figure 6.3). You can access the Find tab from the Replace tab, and vice versa, by clicking the corresponding tab. Then, to find and replace text:

1. In the **Find What** text box, enter the text you want to replace.

2. In the **Replace With** text box, enter the replacement text.

3. Click the **More** button (if necessary) and specify search options as explained in the previous section.

4. Click **Find Next** to locate and highlight the first instance of the target text. Then:

   - Click **Replace** to replace the highlighted instance of the target text, then locate the next instance of it.

- Click **Find Next** to leave the highlighted instance of the target text unchanged and to locate the next instance.

- Click **Replace All** to replace all instances of the target text in the entire document.

 Quick Text Replacement   You can use the AutoCorrect feature, covered in Lesson 18, "Saving Time with AutoCorrect and AutoText," to automatically replace text as you type it.

Figure 6.3   To replace text in your document, use the Replace tab in the Find and Replace dialog box.

 Deleting Text   To delete the target text, follow the previous steps but leave the Replace With text box empty.

 Recovery!   If you make a mistake replacing text, you can recover by clicking **Edit, Undo Replace**.

In this lesson, you learned how to search for and replace text in your document. In the next lesson, "Changing the Screen Display," you will learn about Word's screen display options.

LESSON 7

CHANGING THE SCREEN DISPLAY

In this lesson you learn how to control the Word screen display to suit your working style.

DOCUMENT DISPLAY OPTIONS

Word offers several ways to display your document. Each of these views is designed to make certain editing tasks easier. The available views are

- **Normal View** Best for general editing tasks.

- **Print Layout View** Optimized for fine-tuning the appearance and formatting of a document.

- **Web Layout View** Designed for working with Web documents.

- **Outline View** Designed for working with outlines.

The view you use has no effect on the contents of your document or on the way it will look when printed. It affects only the way the document appears on screen.

NORMAL VIEW

Normal view is suitable for most editing tasks; it is the view you will probably use most often. This is Word's default view. All special formatting is visible onscreen, including different font sizes, italic, boldface, and other enhancements. The screen display is essentially identical to how the document will appear when printed. Certain aspects of the page layout, however, do not appear in order to speed editing; for example, you do not see headers and footers or multiple columns. Figure 7.1 shows a document in Normal view.

 To select Normal view, click **View**, **Normal**, or click the **Normal View** button at the left end of the horizontal scroll bar.

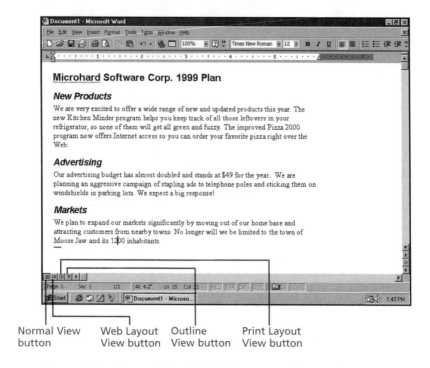

Normal View   Web Layout   Outline   Print Layout
button   View button   View button   View button

Figure 7.1   Normal view is ideal for most editing tasks.

PRINT LAYOUT VIEW

Print Layout view displays your document exactly as it will print. Headers, footers, and all other details of the page layout appear onscreen. You can edit in Print Layout view; it's ideal for fine-tuning the details of page composition. Be aware, however, that the additional processing required in Print Layout view makes display changes relatively slow, particularly when you have a complex page layout. Figure 7.2 shows a sample document in Print Layout view.

Sneak Preview   Use Print Layout view to see what your printed document will look like before you actually print. The Print Preview feature is preferred for previewing entire pages. Whereas Print Layout view permits you to edit the document, however, Print Preview does not.

Header

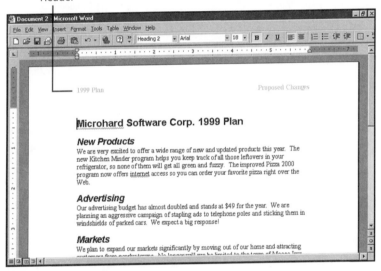

Figure 7.2   A document viewed in Print Layout view shows exactly how the document will print, including headers and footers.

Click **View**, **Print Layout**, or click the **Print Layout View** button at the left end of the horizontal scroll bar to switch to Print Layout view.

WEB LAYOUT VIEW

Web Layout view is designed for editing Web documents. It displays the
document as it will appear when viewed in a Web browser. When you
open a Web document (a file with the HTM or HTML extension), Word
automatically switches to Web Layout view. You can also edit a Web document in Normal view. Figure 7.3 shows a Web document displayed in
Web Layout view.

Use the Proper View   To judge final appearance, use
Print Layout view for documents that will be printed,
and use Web Layout view for documents that will be
published on the Web.

 Click **View, Web Layout,** or click the **Web Layout View** button to switch
to Web Layout view.

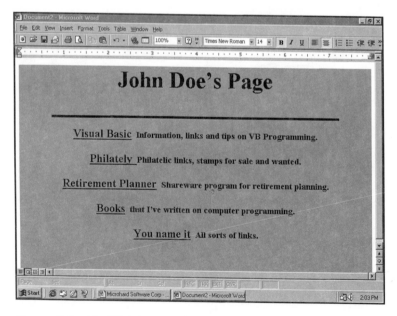

Figure 7.3   Use Web Layout view to preview the appearance of
Web documents.

OUTLINE VIEW

Use Outline view to create outlines and to examine the structure of a document. Figure 7.4 shows a document in Outline view. In this view, you can choose to view only your document headings, thus hiding all subordinate text. You can quickly promote, demote, or move document headings along with subordinate text to a new location. For this view to be useful, you need to assign heading styles to the document headings. (This is discussed in Lesson 14, "Using Styles to Control Formatting.")

Outline toolbar

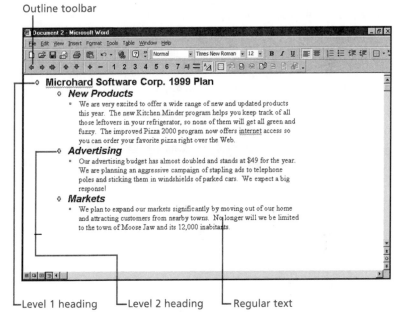

Level 1 heading   Level 2 heading   Regular text

Figure 7.4   Outline view provides a structured display of your document contents and headings.

Click **View, Outline** to switch to Outline view, or click the **Outline View** button at the left end of the horizontal scroll bar.

DRAFT FONT VIEW

Draft Font view is a display option you can apply in both Normal and Outline views. As you can see in Figure 7.5, Draft Font view uses a single generic font for all text; it indicates special formatting by underlining or boldface. Draft Font view provides the fastest editing and screen display, and is particularly useful when editing the content of documents that contain a lot of fancy formatting and large fonts. This view is ideal when you're concentrating on the contents of your document rather than on its appearance.

To turn Draft Font view on or off use the following steps:

1. Click **Tools, Options** to open the Options dialog box.

2. If necessary, click the **View** tab to display the View options.

3. Select the **Draft Font** check box to turn it on or off.

4. Select **OK**.

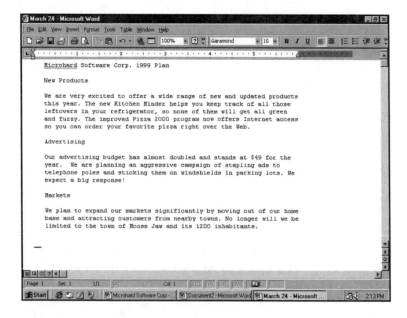

Figure 7.5   Draft Font view displays all text in the same basic font.

FULL SCREEN VIEW

Full Screen view provides the maximum amount of screen real estate to display your document contents. In Full Screen view, the title bar, menu, toolbars, Status bar, and all other Word elements are hidden—your document occupies the entire screen. You use Full Screen view in combination with other views. Thus, you can use Full Screen view in Normal view, Print Layout view, and so on. You can enter and edit text in this view and select from the menus using the usual keyboard commands. Even though the menu is not displayed, you can access it with the mouse by moving the mouse pointer to the top of the screen.

To turn on Full Screen view, click View, **Full Screen.** To turn off Full Screen view, press **Esc** or click the **Close Full Screen** box that appears in the lower-right corner of the screen.

CHANGING THE DOCUMENT DISPLAY SIZE

With the Zoom command, you can control the size of your document on-screen. You can enlarge it to facilitate reading small fonts or decrease it to view an entire page at one time. Click View, **Zoom** to open the Zoom dialog box (see Figure 7.6).

Several options are available in the Zoom dialog box. As you make selections, the Preview area shows you how the selected zoom setting will look. The following options are available in all view settings:

- Select **200%, 100%,** or **75%** to zoom to the indicated magnification. 200% is twice normal size, 75% is three-quarters normal size, and so on.

- Enter a custom magnification in the range 10–200 percent in the Percent text box.

- Select **Text Width** to fit the longest lines of text to the screen width.

- Select **Page Width** to scale the display to fit the entire page width on-screen.

The following settings are available only if you are in Print Layout view:

- Select **Whole Page** to scale the display to fit the entire page, vertically and horizontally, onscreen.

- Select **Many Pages** to display two or more pages at the same time. Click the **Monitor** button located under the Many Pages option, and then drag to specify how many pages to display.

Figure 7.6   Use the Zoom dialog box to change the document display size.

 Quick Zoom   You can quickly change the zoom setting by clicking the **Zoom** drop-down arrow on the Standard toolbar and selecting the desired zoom setting from the list (refer to Figure 7.6).

NAVIGATING QUICKLY WITH THE DOCUMENT MAP

The Document Map is a separate pane that displays your document's headings. You cannot edit in the Document Map; rather, you use it to quickly move around your document. To display the Document Map, or to hide it, click **View, Document Map**. Figure 7.7 shows a document with the map displayed.

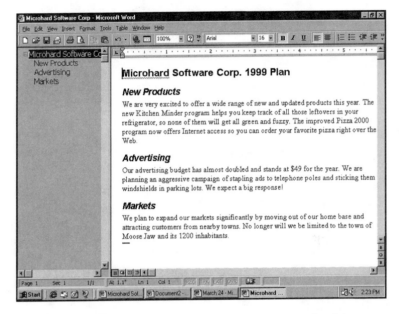

Figure 7.7   The Document Map is displayed to the left of the work area.

To use the document map, simply click the desired map heading, and the main document window scrolls to that location in the document. You can control the width of the map display by pointing at the border between the map and the document and dragging it to the desired location. Dragging the border to the left edge of the screen has the same effect as turning the Document Map off.

SPLITTING THE SCREEN

Word allows you to split the work area into two panels, one above the other, so that you can view different parts of one document at the same time. Each panel scrolls independently and has its own scroll bars. Figure 7.8 shows a document displayed on a split screen. Editing changes that you make in either panel affect the document. To split the screen use the following steps:

1. Click **Window, Split**. Word displays a horizontal splitter bar across the middle of the work area.

2. To accept two equal size panes, click with the left mouse button or press **Enter**. To create different size panes, move the mouse until the splitter bar is in the desired location, then press **Enter**.

You move the editing cursor from one pane to the other by clicking with the mouse. To change the pane sizes, point at the splitter bar and drag it to the new location. To remove the splitter bar and return to regular view, drag the splitter bar to either the top or the bottom of the work area, or click **Windows, Remove Split**.

Keyboard Shortcuts   Press **Ctrl+Alt+S** to toggle the splitter bar on or off.

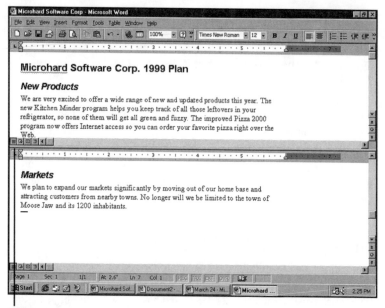

Splitter bar

Figure 7.8   Splitting the screen enables you to view two parts of the same document at once.

Quick Split   You can quickly split the screen by pointing at the splitter bar, just above the up arrow on the vertical toolbar (refer to Figure 7.8), and dragging it down to the desired location.

In this lesson you learned how to control Word's screen display. In the next lesson, "Using Word's Proofreading Tools," you'll learn how to check your documents for errors before printing.

LESSON 8

USING WORD'S PROOFREADING TOOLS

This lesson shows you how to use Word's spelling and grammar checker, thesaurus, and Print Preview window to proof your document.

CHECKING AND CORRECTING SPELLING

Word's spelling checker enables you to verify and correct the spelling of words in your document. Words are checked against a standard dictionary, and unknown words are flagged. You can then ignore the word, correct it, or add it to the dictionary.

To check spelling in a portion of a document, select the text that you want to check. Otherwise, Word checks the entire document, starting at the location of the cursor. If you want the check to start at the beginning of the document, move the insertion point to the start of the document by pressing **Ctrl+Home**. Then use the following steps:

1. Select **Tools, Spelling and Grammar**, or press **F7**. The Spelling and Grammar dialog box appears (see Figure 8.1). If you want to check spelling only, deselect the **Check Grammar** check box. (The remainder of these steps assume that you are checking spelling only.) If you also want to check grammar, Word flags suspected errors; how you deal with these is described later in this lesson.

Toolbar Shortcut To quickly check spelling, click the **Spelling and Grammar** button on the Standard toolbar.

2. When Word locates a word in the document that is not in the dictionary, it displays the word and its surrounding text in the Not In Dictionary box with the word highlighted in red. In Figure 8.1, for example, the word *coud* is highlighted. Suggested replacements for the word appear in the Suggestions box; if Word has no suggestions, this box will be empty. Your options are as follows:

   - To correct the word manually, edit it in the Not In Dictionary box and select **Change**.

   - To use one of the suggested replacements, highlight the desired replacement word in the Suggestions box and select **Change**.

   - To replace all instances of the word in the document with either the manual corrections you made or the word selected in the Suggestions box, select **Change All**.

   - To ignore this instance of the word, select **Ignore**.

   - To ignore this and all other instances of the word in the document, select **Ignore All**.

   - To add the word to the dictionary, select **Add**.

3. Repeat as needed. When the entire document has been checked, Word displays a message to that effect. Or, you can select **Cancel** or **Close** to end spell checking early.

 Personalize Your Dictionary Word flags correctly spelled words, including names, if they are not in the dictionary. By adding such words to the dictionary, they will not be flagged in the future.

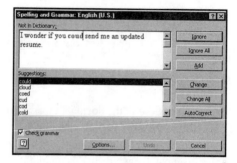

Figure 8.1   Use the Spelling and Grammar dialog box to check and correct spelling in your document.

 Use AutoCorrect To add a misspelled word and its correction to the AutoCorrect list, select AutoCorrect in the Spelling and Grammar dialog box. Future misspellings will then be corrected automatically as you type them. AutoCorrect is covered in Lesson 18, "Saving Time with AutoCorrect and AutoText."

CHECKING YOUR GRAMMAR

Word can check the grammar of the text in your document, flagging possible problems so that you can correct them if necessary. Following are the required steps:

1. Select **Tools, Spelling and Grammar,** or press **F7.** The Spelling and Grammar dialog box appears (refer to Figure 8.1). Make sure the **Check Grammar** check box is selected.

2. When Word locates a word or phrase with a suspected grammatical error, it displays the word or phrase and its surrounding text in the dialog box; the word is highlighted in green and there is a description of the suspected problem above the text. In Figure 8.2, for example, the word *want* is highlighted and the problem

Subject-Verb Agreement appears. Suggested fixes, if any, are listed in the Suggestions list box. Then your options are as follows:

- To manually correct the error, edit the text, then select **Change**.

- To use one of the suggested replacements, select it in the Suggestions list box and select **Change**.

- To ignore this instance of the problem, select **Ignore**.

- To ignore this instance and all other instances of the problem in the document, select **Ignore All**.

3. Word checks spelling at the same time it is checking grammar. Deal with spelling errors as explained earlier in this lesson.

4. Repeat as needed. When the entire document has been checked, Word displays a message to that effect. Or, you can select **Close** to end grammar checking early.

 Don't Rely on Word   Word's grammar checker is a useful tool, but don't rely on it to catch everything. It is no substitute for careful writing and editing.

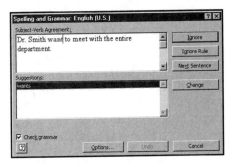

Figure 8.2   Use the Spelling and Grammar dialog box to correct grammatical errors.

CHECKING SPELLING AND GRAMMAR AS YOU TYPE

In addition to checking your document's spelling and grammar all at once, Word can check text as you type. Words not found in the dictionary are underlined with a wavy red line, and suspected grammatical errors are marked with a wavy green line. You can deal with the errors immediately—or whenever you choose. Use the following steps to turn automatic spell/grammar checking on or off:

1. Select **Tools, Options** to open the Options dialog box.

2. If necessary, click the **Spelling and Grammar** tab.

3. Select or deselect the **Check Spelling as You Type** and the **Check Grammar as You Type** check boxes.

4. Click **OK**.

To deal with a word that has been underlined by automatic spell or grammar checking, right-click the word. A pop-up menu appears, containing suggested replacements for the word—if any are found—as well as several commands. Figure 8.3 shows the pop-up menu that appears when you right-click a misspelled word. For a spelling error, your choices are as follows:

- To replace the word with one of the suggestions, click the replacement word.

- To ignore all occurrences of the word in the document, click **Ignore All**.

- To add the word to the dictionary, click **Add**.

- To add the misspelling to the AutoCorrect list, select **AutoCorrect** and then select the proper replacement spelling. Learn more about AutoCorrect in Lesson 18.

- To start a regular spelling check, click **Spelling**.

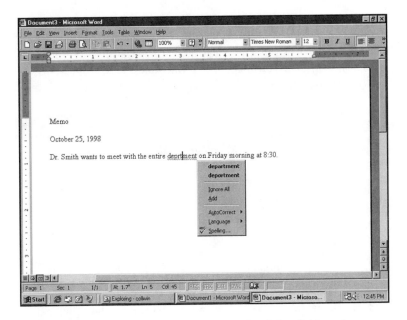

Figure 8.3 Correct spelling as you type by right-clicking the flagged word.

When you right-click a grammatical error, you are offered the following choices:

- To insert a suggested replacement into the document, select it.

- Select **Ignore Sentence** to ignore the possible error.

- Select **Grammar** to start a regular grammar check.

DISPLAYING SPELLING/GRAMMAR MARKS

If your document contains words underlined by the automatic spelling or grammar checker and you want to hide the underlines, select **Tools**, **Options**. On the Spelling and Grammar tab, select the **Hide Spelling Errors in this Document** check box or the **Hide Grammatical Errors in this Document** check box. Deselect these check boxes to redisplay the underlines.

USING THE THESAURUS

A thesaurus provides you with synonyms and antonyms for words in your document. Using the thesaurus can help you express ideas more clearly, avoid repetition in your writing, and improve your vocabulary.

 Synonyms and Antonyms   Words with the same and opposite meanings, respectively, as a given word.

Follow these steps to use the thesaurus:

1. Place the insertion point on the word of interest in your document.

2. Select **Tools**, **Language**, and then **Thesaurus**. Or, you can press **Shift+F7**.

3. The Thesaurus dialog box opens (see Figure 8.4). This dialog box has several components:

   • The Looked Up box displays the word you selected in the document.

   • The Meanings box lists alternative meanings for the word. If the word is not found, Word displays an Alphabetical List box instead; this contains a list of words with spellings similar to the selected word.

   • If the thesaurus finds one or more meanings for the word, the dialog box displays the Replace with Synonym list, which shows synonyms for the currently highlighted meaning of the word. If meanings are not found, the dialog box displays a Replace with Related Word list.

4. While the Thesaurus dialog box is displayed, there are several actions you can take:

   • To find synonyms for the highlighted word in the Replace with Synonym list or the Replace with Related Words list (depending on which one is displayed), select **Look Up**.

- To find synonyms for a word in the Meanings list, select the word and then select **Look Up**.

- For some words, the thesaurus displays the term Antonyms in the Meanings list. To display antonyms for the selected word, highlight the term Antonyms and then select **Look Up**.

5. To replace the word in the document with the highlighted word in the Replace with Synonym list or the Replace with Related Word list, select **Replace**.

6. To close the thesaurus without making any changes to the document, select **Cancel**.

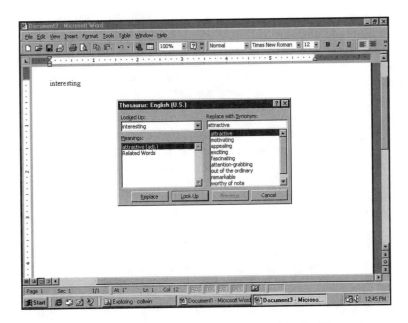

Figure 8.4   You can select an alternative word in the Thesaurus dialog box.

Previewing Your Document's Printer Appearance

Word's Print Preview feature enables you to view your document on the screen exactly as it will be printed. Although Print Layout view also displays your document in its final form, Print Preview offers some additional features that you might find useful. To use Print Preview, select **File, Print Preview,** or click the **Print Preview** button on the Standard toolbar. The current page appears in the Preview window (see Figure 8.5). Then, your choices are as follows:

- To view other pages, press **Page Up** or **Page Down,** or use the scroll bar.

- To view more than one page at a time, click the **Multiple Pages** button, and then drag over the page icons. To return to single page preview, click the **One Page** button.

- To preview the document at different magnifications, click the **Zoom Control** drop-down arrow and select a magnification.

- To display the ruler, click the **View Ruler** button. You can then use the ruler to set page margins and indents as described in Lesson 11, "Applying Indents and Justification," and Lesson 16, "Working with Margins, Pages, and Sections."

- To enlarge the document, click the **Magnifier** button and click in the document. To shrink the view to its original size, click with the right mouse button.

- To prevent a small amount of text from spilling onto the document's last page, click the **Shrink to Fit** button. Word will attempt to adjust formatting to reduce the page count by one.

- To print the document, click the **Print** button.

- To view the preview in full-screen mode, click the **Full Screen** button. Then, to return to normal print preview mode, click the **Close Full Screen** button.

- Click **Close** or press **Esc** to end Print Preview display.

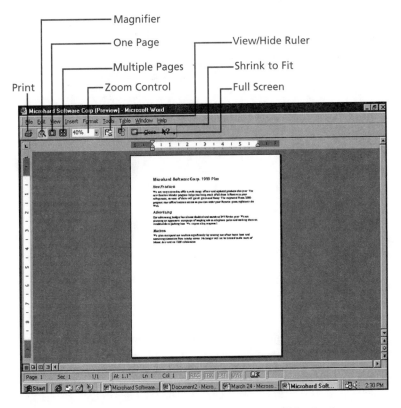

Figure 8.5 You can see how your document will look when printed in the Print Preview window.

In this lesson you learned how to use Word's proofing tools to check your document's spelling and grammar, and how to use the thesaurus and Print Preview. The next lesson, "Printing, Faxing, or Emailing Your Document," shows you how to print, fax, and email your document.

LESSON 9

PRINTING, FAXING, OR EMAILING YOUR DOCUMENT

In this lesson you learn how to print your document, how to send it via email, and how to send a document via fax.

PRINTING USING THE DEFAULT SETTINGS

It's very simple to print using the default settings, which means to print a single copy of the entire document on the default Windows printer. To do so, follow these steps:

1. Click **File, Print**, or press **Ctrl+P**. The Print dialog box appears (see Figure 9.1).

2. Click **OK**. The document prints.

 Quick Printing To print without going to the Print dialog box, click the **Print** button on the Standard toolbar.

 Printer Not Working? Refer to your Microsoft Windows and printer documentation for help. If you're using a network printer, see your network administrator.

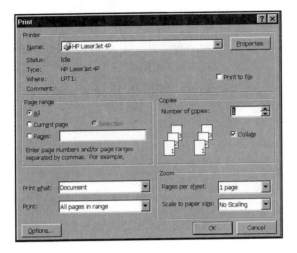

Figure 9.1 To print a document, use the Print dialog box.

PRINTING MULTIPLE COPIES

You can print more than one copy of a document, and you can specify that the copies be collated so that the pages are in the proper order. To print multiple copies, follow these steps:

1. Click **File**, **Print**, or press **Ctrl+P**. The Print dialog box appears (refer to Figure 9.1).

2. In the Number of Copies box, enter the desired number of copies. Or, click the increment arrows to set the desired value.

3. If you want the copies to be collated, select the **Collate** check box to turn it on. Otherwise, turn this option off.

4. Click **OK**.

Don't Use the Wrong Printer If you have two or more printers installed, you can select the one to use by clicking the Name drop-down arrow at the top of the Print dialog box, and then selecting the desired printer from the list.

PRINTING PART OF A DOCUMENT

Most of the time you want to print all of a document. You can, however, print just part of a document, ranging from a single sentence to multiple pages. Follow these steps:

1. To print a section of text, select the text. To print a single page, move the cursor to that page.

2. Click **File, Print,** or press **Ctrl+P**. The Print dialog box appears (refer to Figure 9.1).

3. In the Page Range area, specify what you want to be printed:

   - To print the selected text, choose **Selection**.

   - To print the page containing the cursor, choose **Current Page**.

   - To print specified pages, choose **Pages**, and then enter the page numbers in the text box. For example, entering 1-3 prints pages 1 through 3, entering 2,4 prints pages 2 and 4, and entering 1-5,7,9 prints pages 1 through 5, and pages 7 and 9.

4. Click **OK**.

PRINTING PROPERTIES

To print a document's properties rather than its text, click the **Print What** drop-down arrow in the Print dialog box and select **Document Properties** from the list.

CHANGING YOUR PRINT OPTIONS

Word offers a number of printing options that enable you to tailor the print job to your exact needs. For example, you can print only the odd- or even-numbered pages. Follow these steps:

1. Click **File, Print** to display the Print dialog box (refer to Figure 9.1).

2. Click on the **Print** drop-down list and select **Odd Pages** or **Even Pages**.

3. Click on **OK**.

Printing only the odd- or even-numbered pages is useful in creating two-sided output on a standard one-sided printer: print the odd-numbered pages, and then flip the printed pages over and place them back in the printer's paper tray and print the even-numbered pages.

To set other print options, open the Print dialog box as previously described and click the **Options** button to display the dialog box shown in Figure 9.2.

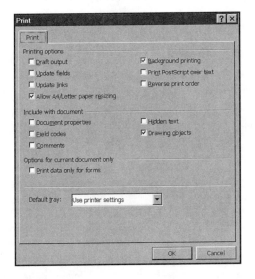

Figure 9.2 Selecting Options from the Print dialog box opens a second Print dialog box for setting advanced printing options.

The options used most often include

• **Draft Output** Produces draft output that prints faster but might lack some graphics and formatting (depending on your specific printer).

- **Reverse Print Order**   Prints pages in last-to-first order. This setting produces collated output on printers that have face-up output.

- **Background Printing**   Permits you to continue working on the document while printing is in progress. This setting uses additional memory and usually results in slower printing.

- **Update Fields**   Updates the contents of all document fields before printing.

- **Document Properties**   Prints the document's properties in addition to its contents.

- **Comments**   Includes document comments in the printout.

After setting the desired printing options, click **OK** to return to the Print dialog box.

Save Time and Paper!   Use Print Layout view to check the appearance of your document before printing it.

FAXING A DOCUMENT

If your system is set up for fax, you can fax a document directly to one or more recipients without having to print a paper copy and feed it into a standard fax machine. You can be set up for fax with a fax modem attached directly to your computer, or via your company's network. This saves both time and paper. To fax the current document, follow these steps:

1. Click **File, Send To,** and then select **Fax Recipient.**

2. Word starts the Fax Wizard, which takes you through the steps of preparing the fax, choosing a cover page, and selecting recipients. After entering the requested information at each step, click **Next.** After the final step, click **Finish.**

3. If you requested a cover sheet, Word displays it. You can make any additions or changes to the cover sheet at this time.

4. Click the **Send Fax Now** button to send the fax.

 No Fax Option?   If the Fax Recipient option is not available on your Send To submenu, it means that your system has not been set up for faxing.

EMAILING A DOCUMENT

If you have Microsoft Messaging or another email program installed on your system, you can send a document directly to a mail recipient. Following are the steps to take:

1. Click **File, Send To, Mail Recipient (as Attachment)**.

2. Depending on the specifics of your system, Word might ask you to select a profile setting. Generally, the default setting is the one that you will select.

3. Next you see your usual New Message window. The appearance of this window varies depending on the mail system you are using, but it will be the same mail form that you use for other email messages. Figure 9.3 shows the New Message window used by Microsoft Outlook Express.

4. The document will already be inserted in the message and represented by an icon, and the message subject line will be filled in (although you can change the subject). You can add text to the message if desired. You must also fill in the To... text box of the message with the recipient's address.

5. When the message is complete, click the **Send** button.

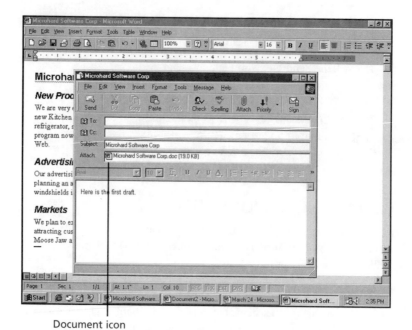

Document icon

Figure 9.3 Word creates a new message with the document inserted as an icon.

When the recipient receives your message, he or she can double-click the document icon to open the document in Word for printing, editing, and so on.

In this lesson, you learned how to print your document and how to send it as a fax or an email message. The next lesson, "Changing the Appearance of Text," shows you how to change the appearance of your text by changing fonts and by using borders and shading in your document.

LESSON 10

CHANGING THE APPEARANCE OF TEXT

In this lesson you learn how to use different fonts, or typefaces, in your document, and how to apply borders and shading.

UNDERSTANDING FONT TERMINOLOGY

Word offers a huge assortment of fonts to use in your documents. Each font has a specific typeface that determines the appearance of the characters. Typefaces are identified by names such as Arial, Courier, and Times New Roman. Each font also has a size, which is specified in points. One point is equal to 1/72 of an inch; so, for example, a 36-point font's largest characters are 1/2-inch tall when printed. Most documents use font sizes in the 8 to 14 point range, but the larger and smaller sizes are available for headings and other special needs.

SELECTING A FONT

You can change the font of text that has already been typed by first selecting the text, and then applying the new font. To specify the font for text you are about to type, simply move the cursor to the desired location. Then follow these steps:

1. Click **Format, Font** to open the Font dialog box (shown in Figure 10.1).

2. The Font list displays the name of the current font. Scroll through the list and select the new font name. The Preview box shows the appearance of the selected font.

3. The Size list displays the current font size. Select the new size from the list or type a number in the text box. The Preview box shows the appearance of the selected font name and size.

4. Select **OK**.

 Quick Select To quickly access the Font dialog box, right-click on selected text and select **Font**.

Select font name — 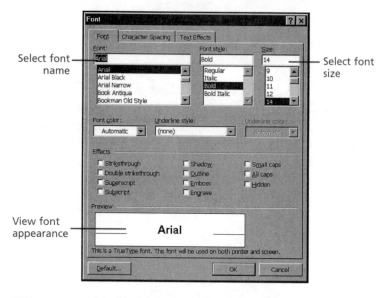 — Select font size

View font appearance

Figure 10.1 Specify the font name and size in the Font dialog box.

You can quickly select a font name and size using the Formatting toolbar. The Font list box and the Font Size list box display the name and size of the current font. You can change the font by clicking the drop-down arrows of either list and making a selection. Note that in the Font list, the fonts you have used recently are placed at the top of the list.

Keyboard Happy? You can use the keyboard to access the Font and Font Size lists on the toolbar by pressing **Ctrl+Shift+F** or **Ctrl+Shift+P** followed by the down arrow. Remember also that you can select an entire document by pressing **Ctrl+A.**

USING BOLDFACE, ITALICS, AND UNDERLINING

You can display any of Word's fonts in boldface, italic, or underline. You can also use a combination of these effects. As with other formatting, you can apply these effects to existing text by first selecting the text, or you can apply them to text you are about to type.

The quickest ways to assign boldface, italics, or underlining are by typing keyboard shortcuts or by clicking the buttons on the Formatting toolbar (see Table 10.1). Click a button to turn the corresponding attribute on; click it again to turn it off. When the cursor is at a location where one of these attributes is turned on, the corresponding toolbar button appears depressed.

TABLE 10.1   COMMAND SHORTCUTS

COMMAND	BUTTON	HOTKEY
Bold	**B**	Ctrl+B
Italic	*I*	Ctrl+I
Underline	<u>U</u>	Ctrl+U

You can also assign font attributes using the Font dialog box. If you want to use underlining other than the default single underline, you must use this method. Use the following steps to do so:

1. Click **Format, Font** to open the Font dialog box (refer to Figure 10.1).

2. Under Font Style, select **Italic**, **Bold Italic**, or **Bold**. Select **Regular** to return to normal text.

3. Click the **Underline** drop-down arrow and select the desired underline style from the list; select **(none)** to remove underlining.

4. Optionally, select the underline color from the Underline Color list.

5. Select **OK**.

A New Default   To change the default font and font size used in documents based on the Normal template, open the Font dialog box; select the desired font, size, and attributes; and click the **Default** button.

APPLYING SPECIAL FONT EFFECTS

Word has a number of special font effects that you can use. These include superscript and subscript, strikethrough, and several graphics effects such as shadow and outline. You can also specify that text be hidden, which means it will not display onscreen or be printed. To assign special font effects to selected text or to text that you are about to type, use the following steps:

1. Click **Format**, **Font** to open the Font dialog box (refer to Figure 10.1).

2. In the Effects area, select the effects that you want. To remove an effect, deselect the check box. The Preview box shows you how the selected effects will look.

3. Select **OK**.

Quick Change Artist   To quickly change capitalization of text, select the text and then press **Shift+F3** one or more times. The text will cycle between no caps, all caps, and initial caps.

Where's That Hidden Text?   To locate hidden text, click **Tools** and then **Options**. On the View tab, select the **Hidden Text** option; hidden text then displays with a dotted underline. You can also display hidden text by clicking the **Show/Hide ¶** button on the Standard toolbar.

ADDING BORDERS TO TEXT

Word's Borders command enables you to improve the appearance of your documents by displaying borders around selected text. Figure 10.2 shows examples of the use of borders. (The figure also illustrates shading, which is covered later in this lesson, in the section "Applying Shading.")

You can apply a border to selected text or to individual paragraphs. To put a border around text, select the text. For a paragraph, place the cursor anywhere in the paragraph. The quickest way to apply a border is to use the Border button on the Formatting toolbar. Click the arrow next to the button to view a palette of available border settings, and then click the desired border diagram. Click the **No Borders** diagram to remove borders.

If you need more control over the appearance of your borders, you must use the Borders and Shading dialog box (see Figure 10.3).

The steps for creating a border are as follows:

1. Select the text to which you want the border applied; or, to place a border around an entire paragraph, position the cursor anywhere in the paragraph.

2. Click **Format**, **Borders and Shading** and then click the **Borders** tab if necessary.

3. Select the general appearance of the borders you want by clicking the corresponding icon in the Setting area. (Use of the Custom setting is explained in the next set of steps.) Select the desired line style from the Style list, the desired line color from the Color list, and the desired line width from the Width list.

4. In the Preview area, click the buttons or click directly on the page diagram to add or remove borders from the four sides of the text.

5. If you selected text before opening the dialog box, use the Apply To list to specify whether you want the border to be displayed around the selected text or the current paragraph.

6. Click **OK**.

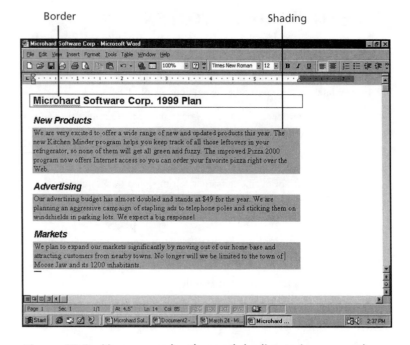

Figure 10.2 You can use borders and shading to improve a document's appearance.

The normal border settings apply the same line style (solid, dotted, and so on) to all four sides of the border box. Use the following steps to create a custom border that combines different styles on different sides:

1. Click the **Custom** icon.

2. Select the line style, color, and width for one side of the border.

3. In the Preview area, click the button or click directly on the page diagram to specify which side of the border you want the style applied to.

4. Repeat steps 2 and 3 to specify the styles for the other three sides of the border.

5. Select **OK**.

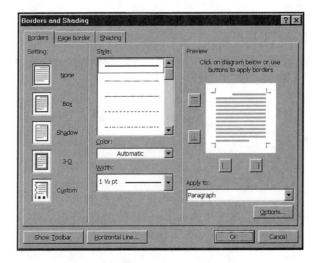

Figure 10.3 Use the Borders tab of the Borders and Shading dialog box to add borders to your text.

You can also place borders around entire pages in your document. To do so, click the **Page Border** tab of the Borders and Shading dialog box. This tab looks and operates just like the Borders tab does in terms of specifying the border's appearance. The only difference is specifying where the border will be applied, which is done with the Apply To list. You have four choices:

- Whole Document
- This Section
- This Section - First Page Only
- This Section - All Except First Page

You'll learn how to divide a document into sections in Lesson 16, "Working with Margins, Pages, and Sections."

APPLYING SHADING

You can use shading to display text over a background color, such as black text on a light gray background. (Figure 10.2 shows an example of shading.) You can apply shading to selected text or to individual paragraphs. Shading is comprised of either a fill color, a pattern color, or a combination of both. Use the following steps to apply shading:

1. Select the text to be shaded, or, to shade an entire paragraph, position the cursor anywhere in the paragraph.

2. Click **Format**, **Borders and Shading** to open the Borders and Shading dialog box. Click the **Shading** tab (see Figure 10.4).

3. To use a fill color, select it from the palette in the Fill area of the dialog box. To use only a pattern color, select **No Fill**.

4. To use a pattern color, select its style and color from the lists in the Patterns section of the dialog box. To use only a fill color, select the **Clear** style. You can view the appearance of the selected settings in the Preview area of the dialog box.

5. If you selected text before opening the dialog box, use the Apply To list to specify whether the fill will apply to the selected text or to the current paragraph.

6. Select **OK**.

 Printing Color?   Of course, color shading prints in color only if you have a color printer. You need to perform test printouts of pages with shading because screen display of shading is often quite different from the final printed results.

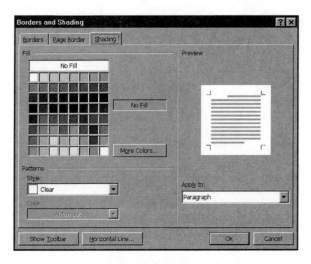

Figure 10.4 To apply shading to your document, use the Shading tab of the Borders and Shading dialog box.

This lesson showed you how to use fonts, borders, and shading in your documents. The next lesson, "Applying Indents and Justification," teaches you how to control indentation and justification of text, and how to control line breaks.

LESSON 11

APPLYING INDENTS AND JUSTIFICATION

In this lesson, you learn how to set the indentation and justification of text in your document, and how to control line breaks.

CHANGING INDENTATION

The distance between your text and the left and right edges of the page is controlled by two things: the left and right page margins and the text indentation. Margins, which are covered in Lesson 16, "Working with Margins, Pages, and Sections," are usually changed only for entire documents or for large sections of a document. For smaller sections of text, such as individual lines and paragraphs, use indentation.

Indentation The distance between a paragraph's text and the margins for the entire document. For example, if the left margin is set at one inch and a paragraph has a one-inch indentation, that paragraph starts two inches from the edge of the paper.

The easiest way to set indents is by using the Ruler and your mouse. To display the Ruler (or to hide it), click **View, Ruler**. The numbers on the Ruler indicate the space from the left margin in inches. Figure 11.1 shows the Ruler and identifies the elements used to set indents. It also illustrates the various indent options.

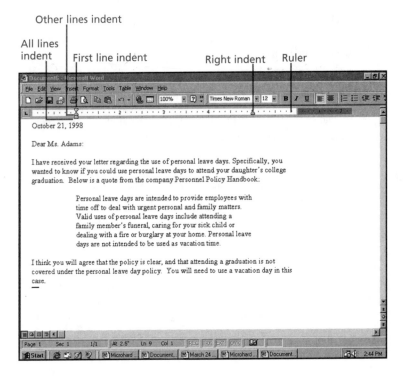

Figure 11.1 Using the Ruler to set text indentation, the second paragraph is indented one inch from both the right and left margins.

Indentation applies to individual paragraphs. To set indentation for one paragraph, position the cursor anywhere in the paragraph. For more than one paragraph, select the paragraphs. Then drag the indent markers on the Ruler to the desired positions. As you drag, a dotted vertical line displays down the document to show the new indent location. If you don't select paragraphs or place the cursor in a single paragraph, the new indents will apply only to new paragraphs that you type from the insertion point forward. There are several ways in which you can change indentation:

- To change the indent of the first line of a paragraph, drag the **First Line Indent** marker to the desired position.

- To change the indent of all lines of a paragraph, except the first one, drag the **Other Lines Indent** marker to the desired position (this is called a hanging indent).

- To change the indent of all lines of a paragraph, drag the **All Lines Indent** marker to the desired position.

- To change the indent of the right edge of the paragraph, drag the **Right Indent** marker to the desired position.

You can also quickly increase or decrease (by 1/2 inch) the left indent of the current paragraph by clicking the **Increase Indent** or **Decrease Indent** buttons on the Formatting toolbar. The quickest way to indent the first line of a paragraph is to position the cursor at the start of the line and press **Tab**.

Can't Find Toolbar Buttons?   To find hidden toolbar buttons, click the More Buttons button on the Formatting toolbar. To learn about toolbars, refer to Lesson 1, "Getting Started with Microsoft Word."

Rapid Ruler   Quickly display the Ruler by positioning the mouse pointer at the top edge of the work area for a moment. After you're done using the Ruler and move the mouse pointer away, the Ruler is automatically hidden again.

Hanging Indent   A paragraph in which the first line is indented less than all the other lines.

SETTING INDENTS WITH THE PARAGRAPHS DIALOG BOX

Word also gives you the option of setting indents using the Paragraph dialog box:

1. Click **Format, Paragraph** to open the Paragraph dialog box, then click the **Indents and Spacing** tab if necessary to display the indents and spacing options (see Figure 11.2).

2. Under Indentation, click the increment arrows of the Left or Right text boxes to increase or decrease the indentation settings. For a first line or a hanging indent, select the indent type in the Special drop-down list, and then enter the indent amount in the By text box. The sample page in the dialog box illustrates the appearance of the current settings.

3. Click **OK**. The new settings are applied to any selected paragraphs or to new text.

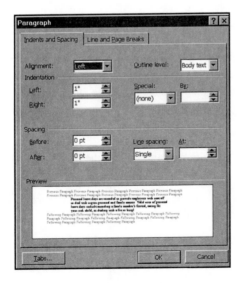

Figure 11.2 You can set indents to exact values in the Paragraph dialog box.

SETTING TEXT JUSTIFICATION

Justification, sometimes called alignment, refers to the manner in which the left and right ends of lines of text are aligned. Word offers four justification options:

- Left justification aligns the left ends of lines.

- Right justification aligns the right ends of lines.

- Full justification aligns both the left and right ends of lines.

- Center justification centers lines between the left and right margins.

 Full Justification   Both the left and right edges of paragraphs are aligned, like a column of text in a newspaper. Word accomplishes full justification by inserting extra space between words and letters in the text as needed.

Figure 11.3 illustrates the justification options. To change the justification for one or more paragraphs, first select the paragraphs, and then click one of the justification buttons on the Formatting toolbar.

If you prefer to use a dialog box to change justification, select the paragraphs, and then:

1. Click **Format, Paragraph** to open the Paragraph dialog box, and click the **Indents and Spacing** tab if necessary.

2. Click the **Alignment** drop-down arrow and select the desired alignment from the list.

3. Select **OK**.

 How Is It Justified?   The toolbar button corresponding to the current paragraph's justification setting appears depressed.

Align right

Align center

Align left   Justify

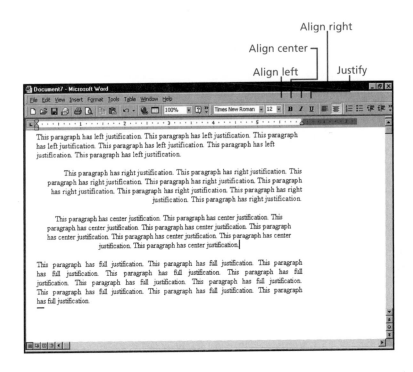

Figure 11.3   To set text justification, click an alignment button.

CONTROLLING LINE BREAKS

 Line Break   Where text ends at the right margin and begins on the next line at the left margin.

The word wrap feature automatically breaks each line of text when it reaches the right margin. This might not always be what you want, however. Word offers a couple of methods for controlling the way lines break. You can, for example, prevent a line break from occurring between two specific words, thus ensuring that the words always remain together on the same line. These methods can be particularly useful when you modify indents and justification because this often changes where individual lines break.

Word's default is to break lines as needed at spaces or hyphens. To prevent a line break, you must insert a non-breaking space or a non-breaking hyphen instead. To insert a non-breaking hyphen, press **Ctrl+Shift+-** (hyphen). To insert a non-breaking space, press **Ctrl+Shift+spacebar**.

You can also use an optional hyphen to specify where a word can be broken, if necessary. This is useful with long words that might fall at the end of the line; if word wrap moves the long word to the next line, there will be an unsightly gap at the end of the previous line. An optional hyphen remains hidden unless the word extends past the right margin. If this happens, the hyphen appears and only the part of the word after the hyphen wraps to the new line. To insert an optional hyphen, press **Ctrl+-** (hyphen).

Finally, you can insert a line break without starting a new paragraph by pressing **Shift+Enter**.

In this lesson, you learned how to set the indentation and justification of text in your document, and how to control line breaks. The next lesson, "Creating Numbered and Bulleted Lists," shows you how to create numbered and bulleted lists.

LESSON 12

CREATING NUMBERED AND BULLETED LISTS

This lesson shows you how to add numbered and bulleted lists to your documents.

WHY USE NUMBERED AND BULLETED LISTS?

Numbered and bulleted lists are useful formatting tools for setting off lists of information in a document—you've seen plenty of both in this book! Word can automatically create both types of lists. Use bulleted lists for items that consist of related information, but are in no particular order. Use numbered lists for items with a specific order. When you create a numbered or bulleted list, each paragraph is considered a separate list item and automatically receives its own number or bullet.

CREATING A NUMBERED OR BULLETED LIST

You can either create a list from existing text, or create the list as you type. To create a numbered or bulleted list from existing text, follow these steps:

1. Select the paragraphs you want in the list.

2. Click **Format, Bullets and Numbering** to open the Bullets and Numbering dialog box.

3. Depending on the type of list you want, click the **Bulleted** tab or the **Numbered** tab. Figure 12.1 shows the Numbered tab options, and Figure 12.2 shows the Bulleted tab options.

4. Click the bullet or number style you want.

5. Select **OK**.

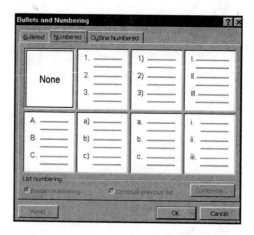

Figure 12.1   Select numbered list style options in the Numbered tab.

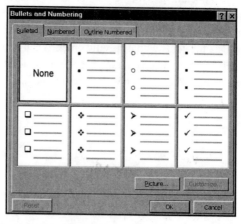

Figure 12.2   Select bulleted list style options in the Bulleted tab.

To create a numbered or bulleted list as you type

1. Move the insertion point to the location for the list. Press **Enter**, if necessary, to start a new paragraph.

2. Select **Format**, **Bullets and Numbering** to open the Bullets and Numbering dialog box.

3. Depending on the type of list you want, click the **Bulleted** tab or the **Numbered** tab.

4. Click the bullet or number style you want.

5. Select **OK**.

6. Type the list elements, pressing **Enter** at the end of each paragraph. Each new paragraph is automatically numbered or bulleted as it is added.

7. At the end of the last paragraph, press **Enter** twice.

 Quick Lists   Quickly create a numbered or bulleted list in the default list style by clicking the **Numbering** or **Bullets** button on the Formatting toolbar either before typing or after selecting the list text. To learn more about toolbar buttons, refer to Lesson 1, "Getting Started with Microsoft Word."

 Automatic Lists   If the corresponding AutoFormat options are on, Word automatically starts a numbered or bulleted list if you start a paragraph with a number and period or an asterisk followed by a space or tab. To turn these options on or off, click **Format**, **AutoFormat**, and then **Options** and turn the **Lists** and the **Automatic Bulleted Lists** check boxes on or off.

USING MULTILEVEL LISTS

A multilevel list contains two or more levels of bullets or numbering within a single list. For example, a numbered list might contain a lettered list under each numbered item, or each level might be numbered separately, as in an outline. Here's how to create a multilevel list:

1. Click **Format, Bullets and Numbering** to open the Bullets and Numbering dialog box.

2. Click the **Outline Numbered** tab to display the multilevel options, as shown in Figure 12.3.

3. Click the list style you want, then click **OK**.

4. Start typing the list, pressing **Enter** after each item.

5. After pressing **Enter**, either press **Tab** to demote the new item one level, or **Shift+Tab** to promote it one level. Otherwise, the new item will be at the same level as the previous item.

6. After typing the last item, press **Enter**, and then click the **Numbering** button on the Formatting toolbar to end the list.

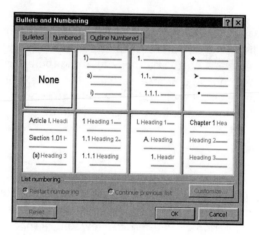

Figure 12.3 Use the Outline Numbered tab of the Bullets and Numbering dialog box to create a multilevel list.

You can convert regular text or a one-level numbered or bulleted list to a multilevel list. You can also change the style of an existing multilevel list. The steps are as follows:

1. Select all the paragraphs that are to be in the new list or whose format you want to modify.

2. Click **Format, Bullets and Numbering**, and then click the **Outline Numbered** tab.

3. Click the desired list style, then click **OK**.

4. Move the insertion point to an item in the list whose level you want to change.

5. Click the **Decrease Indent** or **Increase Indent** buttons on the Formatting toolbar to change the item's level.

6. Repeat steps 4 and 5 as needed to change other items.

REMOVING NUMBERING OR BULLETS FROM A LIST

Follow these steps to remove bullets or numbers from a list while keeping the text and converting it to normal paragraphs:

1. Select the paragraphs from which you want the bullets or numbering removed. This can be the entire list or just part of it. The corresponding button (Bullets or Numbering) on the Formatting toolbar appears depressed.

2. Click the **Bullets** or **Numbering** button. If only a portion of a numbered list was selected, the other numbers change to reflect the edit.

CHANGING THE FORMAT OF A NUMBERED OR BULLETED LIST

You can also change the format of an existing bulleted or numbered list; to change the bullet symbol or the numbering style, use the following steps:

1. Select the paragraphs whose bullet or numbering style you want to change. This can be the entire list or just part of it. Formatting changes made to part of a numbered list are reflected in the entire list, but changes made to bullet formatting only affect those bullets selected.

2. Select **Format, Bullets and Numbering** to open the Bullets and Numbering dialog box.

3. For a bulleted list, click the **Bulleted** tab and select the desired style. Select **None** to remove bullets.

4. For a numbered list, click the **Numbered** tab and select the desired numbering style, or click **None** to remove numbering from the list.

5. Select **OK**.

ADDING ITEMS TO NUMBERED AND BULLETED LISTS

You can add new items to a numbered or bulleted list as follows:

1. Move the insertion point to the location in the list where you want the new item.

2. Press **Enter** to start a new paragraph. Word automatically inserts a new bullet or number, and renumbers the list items as needed.

3. Type the new text.

4. If it's a multilevel list, click the **Decrease Indent** and **Increase Indent** buttons on the Formatting toolbar to change the item's level, if desired.

5. Repeat as many times as needed.

This lesson showed you how to create numbered and bulleted lists. The next lesson, "Setting Tabs and Line Spacing," shows you how to use tabs and change line spacing.

Lesson 13

Setting Tabs and Line Spacing

In this lesson, you learn how to use and set tab stops and how to change line spacing.

What Are Tabs?

Tabs provide a way for you to control the indentation and vertical alignment of text in your document. When you press the Tab key, Word inserts a tab in the document; this moves the cursor—and any text to the right of it—to the next tab stop. By default, Word has tab stops at 1/2-inch intervals across the width of the page. You can modify the location of tab stops and control the way text aligns at a tab stop.

Types of Tab Stops

There are four types of tab stops, and each aligns text differently:

- **Left-aligned**   The left edge of text aligns at the tab stop. Word's default tab stops are left-aligned.

- **Right-aligned**   The right edge of text aligns at the tab stop.

- **Center-aligned**   The text is centered at the tab stop.

- **Decimal-aligned**   The decimal point (period) is aligned at the tab stop. You use this type of tab for aligning columns of numbers.

Figure 13.1 illustrates the effects of the four tab alignment options and shows the four markers that appear on the ruler to indicate the positions of the tab stops.

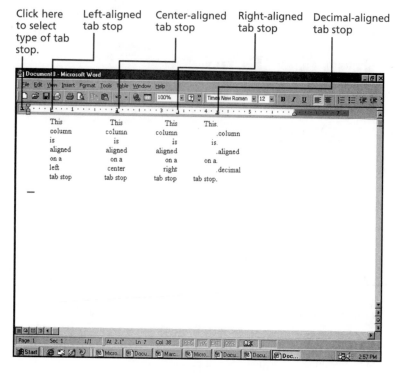

Figure 13.1 Word offers you these four tab stop alignment options.

CHANGING THE DEFAULT TAB STOPS

Default tab stops affect all paragraphs for which you have not set custom tabs. (This is covered in the next section.) The default tab stop spacing affects the entire document. You cannot delete the default tab stops, but you can change the spacing between them. Following are the steps to change the positioning of the tabs:

1. Click **Format**, **Tabs** to display the Tabs dialog box, as shown in Figure 13.2.

2. In the Default Tab Stops box, click the increment arrows to increase or decrease the spacing between default tab stops.

3. Click **OK**.

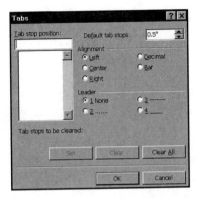

Figure 13.2   You can set tab spacing and alignment in the Tabs dialog box.

   Good-bye Tabs   To effectively "delete" all the default tab stops, set the spacing between them to a value larger than the page width.

CREATING CUSTOM TAB STOPS

If the default tab stops sare not suited to your needs, you can add custom tab stops. The number, spacing, and type of custom tab stops is entirely up to you:

1. Select the paragraphs that will have custom tabs. If no text is selected, the new tabs affect the paragraph containing the cursor and the new text you type.

2. Click the **tab** symbol at the left end of the ruler until it displays the marker for the type of tab you want to insert (refer to Figure 13.1 for the different tab symbols).

3. Point at the approximate tab stop location on the ruler, and press and hold the left mouse button. A dashed vertical line extends down through the document showing the tab stop position relative to your text.

4. Move the mouse left or right until the tab stop is at the desired location.

5. Release the mouse button.

 No Ruler?   If your ruler is not displayed, click **View**, **Ruler** or position the mouse pointer near the top edge of the work area for a few seconds and the ruler will appear.

When you add a custom tab stop, all the default tab stops to the left are temporarily inactivated. This ensures that the custom tab stop will take precedence. If custom tabs have been defined for the current paragraph, then the custom tabs are displayed on the ruler; otherwise, the default tab stops are displayed as thin lines in the lower border of the ruler.

MOVING AND DELETING CUSTOM TAB STOPS

Follow these steps to move a custom tab stop to a new position:

1. Point at the **tab stop** marker on the ruler.

2. Press and hold the left mouse button.

3. Drag the tab stop to the new position.

4. Release the mouse button.

To delete a custom tab stop, follow the same steps, but, in step 3, drag the **tab stop** marker off the ruler, and then release the mouse button.

CHANGING LINE SPACING

Line spacing controls the amount of vertical space between lines of text. Different spacing is appropriate for different kinds of documents. If you want to print your document on as few pages as possible, use single line

spacing to position lines close together. In contrast, a document that will
later be edited by hand ought to be printed with wide line spacing to provide space for the editor to write comments.

Word offers a variety of line spacing options. If you change line spacing,
it affects the selected text; if there is no text selected, it affects the current
paragraph and text you type at the insertion point. To change line spacing:

1. Click **Format, Paragraph** to open the Paragraph dialog box. If
   necessary, click the **Indents and Spacing** tab (see Figure 13.3).

2. Click the **Line Spacing** drop-down arrow and select the desired
   spacing from the list. The **Single, 1.5 Lines,** and **Double** settings
   are self-explanatory. The other settings are

   - **Exactly**   Space between lines will be exactly the value,
     in points, that you enter in the At text box.

   - **At Least**   Space between lines will be at least the value
     you enter in the At text box; Word increases the spacing as
     needed if the line contains large characters.

   - **Multiple**   Changes spacing by the factor you enter in the
     At text box. For example, enter 1.5 to increase spacing
     by one and a half times, and enter 2 to double the line
     spacing.

Underline Missing?   If you set line spacing—using the
Exactly option—at the same value as your font size,
then the underline displays only for the last line of
each paragraph.

3. To add spacing before the first line, or after the last line, of the
   paragraph, enter the desired space (in points) or click the increment arrows in the Before and After text boxes.

4. View the appearance of the selected options in the Preview box.

5. Click **OK**.

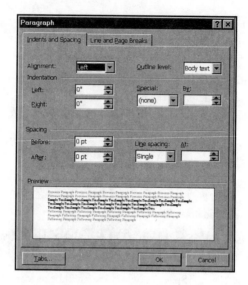

Figure 13.3 You set line spacing in the Indents and Spacing tab of the Paragraph dialog box.

In this lesson, you learned how to set and use tab stops and how to change line spacing. The next lesson, "Using Styles to Control Formatting," shows you how to use styles to simplify your text formatting tasks.

LESSON 14

USING STYLES TO CONTROL FORMATTING

In this lesson you learn how to use styles in your documents to simplify formatting tasks.

UNDERSTANDING STYLES

Word's styles provide a great deal of power and flexibility when it comes to formatting your document. A *style* is a collection of formatting specifications that has been assigned a name and saved. For example, a given style can specify 14-point Arial font, one inch indent, double line spacing, and full justification. After you define a style, you can quickly apply it to any text in your document. Applying a style is much faster than manually applying individual formatting elements and has the added advantage of assuring consistency. If you later modify a style definition, all the text in the document to which that style has been assigned automatically changes to reflect the new style formatting. Word has several predefined styles, but you can also create your own.

 What Is a Style? A style is a named collection of paragraph and character formatting that can be reused.

Word has two types of styles:

- **Paragraph styles** Apply to entire paragraphs, and can include all aspects of formatting that affect a paragraph's appearance: font, line spacing, indents, tab stops, borders, and so on. Every paragraph has a style; the default paragraph style is called Normal.

- **Character styles** Apply to any section of text, and can include any formatting that applies to individual characters— font name and size, underlining, boldface, and so on. In other words, these include any of the formats that you can assign by clicking **Format, Font**. There is no default character style.

When you apply a character style, the formatting is applied in addition to whatever formatting the text already possesses. For example, if you apply a character style defined as boldface to a sentence that is already format-ted as italic, the word displays in boldface italic. The uses of styles are covered in this lesson and the next one.

ASSIGNING A STYLE TO TEXT

To assign a paragraph style to multiple paragraphs, select the paragraphs. To assign a paragraph style to a single paragraph, place the cursor any-where inside the paragraph. To assign a character style, select the text you want the style to affect, and then:

1. Click the **Style** drop-down arrow on the Formatting toolbar to see a list of available styles with each style name displayed in the style's font. In addition to font size and justification, symbols in the list also indicate whether a style is a paragraph or charac-ter style (see Figure 14.1).

Can't Find the Style List? You might need to slide the divider between the Standard and Formatting toolbars to make the Style list visible. Learn more about toolbars in Lesson 1, "Getting Started with Microsoft Word."

2. Select the desired style by clicking its name. The style is applied to the specified text.

 Paragraph or Character Style? In the Style list, paragraph styles are listed with the paragraph symbol next to them and character styles have an underlined letter *a* next to them.

To remove a character style from text, select the text and apply the character style Default Paragraph Font. This is not really a style; rather, it specifies that the formatting defined in the current paragraph style should be used for the text.

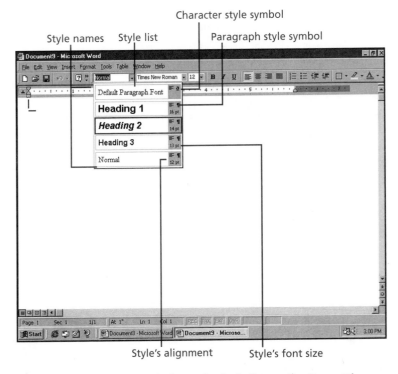

Figure 14.1   Select a style from the Style list on the Formatting toolbar.

VIEWING STYLE NAMES

The Style list on the Formatting toolbar displays the name of the style assigned to the text at the insertion point. If there is text selected or if the insertion point is in text that has a character style applied, then the Style list displays the character style name. Otherwise, it displays the paragraph style of the current paragraph.

Word can also display the name of the paragraph and character styles assigned to specific text in your document:

1. Press **Shift+F1** or click **Help**, **What's This** to activate What's This Help. The mouse cursor displays a question mark.

2. Click the text of interest. Word displays a balloon containing information about the text's style assignment, as shown in Figure 14.2.

3. Repeat step 2 as needed for other text.

4. Press **Esc** when you are finished.

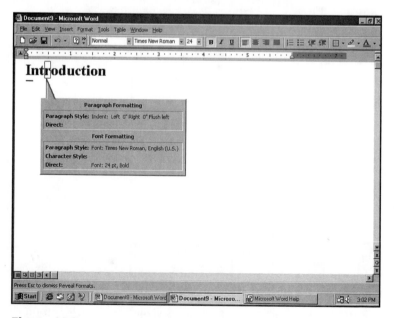

Figure 14.2   Display text style information with What's This Help.

CREATING A NEW STYLE

You are not limited to using Word's predefined styles. In fact, creating your own styles is an essential part of getting the most out of Word's style capabilities. You can create a new paragraph style by using the following steps:

1. Find a paragraph to which you want to apply the new style.

2. Format the paragraph as desired. In other words, apply the formatting you want included in the new style definition: font, indents, line spacing, and so on.

3. With the insertion point anywhere in the paragraph, click in the **Style** drop-down list (not its arrow) to highlight the current style name.

4. Type the new style name, which replaces the current style name, and press **Enter**.

In step 4, don't enter the name of an existing style. If you do, that style's formatting is applied to the paragraph and the formatting changes you made are lost. If this happens, you can recover the formatting by clicking **Edit, Undo**, then repeating steps 3 and 4 with a new style name.

You can also create a new style by making formatting entries in dialog boxes. You must use this method to create a character style; it is optional for paragraph styles. You can either create a new style from scratch or base it on an existing style. If you choose the latter method, the new style has all the formatting of the base style plus any additions and changes you make when defining the style. Following are the required steps:

1. Click **Format, Style** to open the Style dialog box.

2. Click the **New** button. The New Style dialog box appears (see Figure 14.3).

3. Click the **Style Type** drop-down arrow and select **Character** or **Paragraph** from the list, depending on the type of style you're creating.

4. Click the **Name** text box and type the name for the new style. Use a descriptive name if possible, such as Bold Indented.

5. If you want to base the new style on an existing style other than Normal, click the **Based On** drop-down arrow and select the desired base style from the list.

6. If you want the new style to be part of the template that the current document is based on, select the **Add to Template** check box. If you do not select this check box, the new style will be available only in the current document. If the current document is based on the Normal Template, as most documents are, then the style is available to all the documents you begin with the default Normal Template.

7. The **Automatically Update** check box is available only for paragraph styles. When this option is selected, any formatting changes you make to a paragraph that has this style assigned cause Word to automatically update the paragraph style definition to include the changes.

8. To specify the font or border of the new style, click the **Format** button and select **Font** or **Border**. As you make format changes, the Preview box displays an image of how the style will look and the Description area provides a description of the style elements.

9. To set the style's indents, line spacing, and tabs, click the **Format** button and select **Paragraph** (to set indents and line spacing) or select **Tabs**. This step applies to paragraph styles only.

10. Click **OK** to return to the Style dialog box.

11. Click **Apply** to assign the new style to the current text or paragraph. Click **Close** to save the new style definition without assigning it to any text.

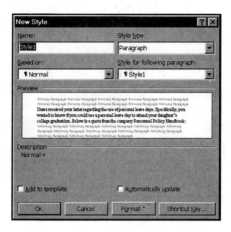

Figure 14.3   You can create custom styles in the New Style dialog box.

MODIFYING A STYLE

You can change the formatting associated with any paragraph or character style—it can be a style you define or one of Word's predefined styles. When you do so, all text in the document that has the style assigned is modified to reflect the new formatting. Here's how:

1. Click **Format, Style** to open the Style dialog box (see Figure 14.4).

2. Click the **List** drop-down arrow and select which styles you want to be displayed in the Styles list:

   - **All Styles**   All styles defined in the current document.

   - **Styles in Use**   Styles that have been assigned to text in the current document.

   - **User Defined Styles**   All user-defined styles in the current document (as opposed to those styles provided by Word).

3. In the Styles list, click the name of the style you want to modify.

4. Click the **Modify** button. The Modify Style dialog box appears, which looks the same as the New Style dialog box (refer to Figure 14.3).

5. In this dialog box, specify the style's new format specifications (as described earlier) for creating a new style.

6. Click **OK** to return to the Style dialog box, then click **Close**.

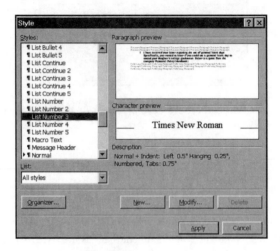

Figure 14.4   Use the Style dialog box to modify an existing style.

In this lesson you learned what styles are, how to apply styles to text, and how to create and modify styles. The next lesson, "Advanced Style Techniques," shows you some advanced style techniques.

LESSON 15

ADVANCED STYLE TECHNIQUES

In this lesson you learn how to assign styles automatically, how to use the heading styles in Outline view, and how to specify spacing between paragraphs. You also learn how to assign shortcut keys to styles and how to find and replace styles.

AUTOMATIC STYLE ASSIGNMENT

When you press **Enter** to start a new paragraph, Word normally assigns to the new paragraph the same style that is assigned to the previous paragraph. There might be times, however, when you want paragraphs of a certain style to always be followed by a differently styled paragraph. For example, say you have created a Section Heading style. Because a section heading is never followed by another section heading, but rather by regular text, save yourself time and effort by specifying that paragraphs with the Section Heading style always be followed by a paragraph with the Normal style. Only paragraph styles can be automatically assigned in this way. Here's how:

1. Click **Format, Style** to open the Style dialog box. If necessary, select the desired paragraph style in the Styles list.

2. Click the **Modify** button to open the Modify Style dialog box (see Figure 15.1).

3. Click the **Style for Following Paragraph** drop-down arrow and select the style you want assigned automatically to the following paragraphs.

4. Click **OK** to return to the Style dialog box, and then click **Close**.

Figure 15.1   Set automatic style assignments in the Modify Style dialog box.

When you specify one style to always follow another, it does not affect existing paragraphs in your document. Only new paragraphs are affected as they are added.

USING WORD'S HEADING STYLES IN OUTLINE VIEW

Word's predefined styles include nine heading styles, named Heading 1 through Heading 9; they can be very useful in certain kinds of documents. In addition to being used as regular styles for assigning formatting to text, Headings 1–7 are used in Word's Outline view, which you learned about in Lesson 7, " Changing the Screen Display." In Outline view, each heading style is automatically applied as an outline level, with Heading 1 as the top level, Heading 2 as the next level, and so on through Heading 7. Figure 15.2 shows a document in Outline view with headings displayed.

Only Three Headings Are Listed   By default, the Styles list on the Formatting toolbar displays only headings 1–3. To assign other heading levels, use Outline view (as explained later in this chapter). You can also click Format, Style to display the Style dialog box. Under List, select All Styles, and then select the desired style from the Styles list.

 Outline View   To switch to Outline view, click the Outline View button or click View, Outline.

Promote or   Move heading
demote a   up or down in   Expand or collapse
heading   the document   a heading

Microhard Software Corp. 1999 Plan

New Products
- We are very excited to offer a wide range of new and updated products this year. The new Kitchen Minder program helps you keep track of all those leftovers in your refrigerator, so none of them will get all green and fuzzy. The improved Pizza 2000 program now offers Internet access so you can order your favorite pizza right over the Web.

Advertising
- Our advertising budget has almost doubled and stands at $49 for the year. We are planning an aggressive campaign of stapling ads to telephone poles and sticking them on windshields in parking lots. We expect a big response!

Markets
- We plan to expand our markets significantly by moving out of our home base and attracting customers from nearby towns. No longer will we be limited to the town of Moose Jaw and its 1200 inhabitants.

Drag to move, promote,   Select levels   Show first
or demote a heading   to view   line only

Figure 15.2   A document with headings displays as an outline in Outline view.

In Outline view, you can display headings only or you can display both headings and normal text. When showing headings, you can specify which levels are displayed and which are hidden. You can also promote and demote headings, which changes them to a higher or lower heading level. When you promote or demote a heading, all its subheads are promoted or demoted the same number of levels. You can also move headings around in the document, and all the subheadings and text are moved too. You can expand a heading to display the text that follows it, and then collapse it to hide the text again.

In Outline view, each heading has a plus sign next to it if it contains subheadings or text, and a minus sign if it does not. You work with outlines by using these symbols and the Outline toolbar, shown in Figure 15.2. Following is a list of the things you can do in Outline view:

- To promote a heading, drag its symbol to the left and click the **Promote** button, or press **Shift+Tab**.

- To demote a heading, drag its symbol to the right and click the **Demote** button, or press **Tab**.

- To move a heading to a different location in the document, drag its symbol up or down or click the **Move** buttons.

- To expand or collapse a heading, click the **Expand** or **Collapse** button.

- To view headings with only the first line of following text, click the **Show First Line Only** button.

- To control which levels are displayed, click one of the level buttons. For example, click **4** to display levels 1–4 and hide lower levels and normal text. Click **All** to display all levels plus normal text.

In Outline view, you can edit text, assign styles, and perform other editing tasks in the usual manner. Aside from their use in Outline view, the Heading styles are just like any other style. You can modify the style formatting any way you want.

Style Might Determine the Level   If you assign a paragraph style that has an outline level, whatever text you assigned it to is locked into that outline level—you can't demote or promote it. You have to first assign a style that doesn't have an outline level, and then you can change the level of the text.

AUTOMATIC SPACING BETWEEN PARAGRAPHS

The appearance of your documents improves if some blank space is left between the end of one paragraph and the start of the next. You can accomplish this by pressing **Enter** twice at the end of a paragraph, in effect inserting a blank line between paragraphs. By using styles, you can not only have greater control over your paragraph spacing—you can save time, too. Following are the steps:

1. Click **Format, Style** to open the Style dialog box. Select the desired paragraph style in the Styles list.

2. Click **Modify** to open the Modify Style dialog box.

3. Click the **Format** button, and then choose **Paragraph** from the list that appears. The Paragraph dialog box opens (see Figure 15.3).

4. If necessary, click the **Indents and Spacing** tab.

5. In the Spacing area, enter the desired spacing or click the increment arrows in the **Before** text box (for space preceding the paragraph) or the **After** text box (for space following the paragraph).

6. Click **OK** twice, and then click **Close**. Paragraphs in the selected style now automatically have the specified amount of blank space preceding or following them.

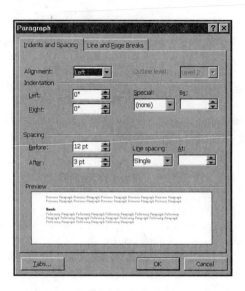

Figure 15.3　You set spacing between paragraphs in the Paragraph dialog box.

The units used to specify the spacing before or after a paragraph are points, the same unit that is used to specify font size. Remember, a point is 1/72 of an inch. To have approximately one line of spacing before or after a paragraph, enter a value equal to the point size of the paragraph style's font.

Assigning Shortcut Keys to Styles

If you use some styles frequently, or if you prefer to use the keyboard rather than the mouse, you can assign shortcut key combinations to styles. Then all you need to do to assign the style is press the specified keys. Here's how to do it:

1. Click **Format, Style** to open the Style dialog box. Select the desired style in the Styles list.

2. Click **Modify** to open the Modify Style dialog box.

3. Click the **Shortcut Key** button to open the Customize Keyboard dialog box (see Figure 15.4).

4. Press the key combination you want assigned to the style. The Press New Shortcut Key box displays a description of the keys you pressed. Just below this box, Word indicates if the shortcut key already has an assigned style/command or if it is unassigned.

5. To accept the shortcut key, click the **Assign** button. To enter a different shortcut key, press **Backspace** to erase the key, and then return to step 4.

6. Click **Close** to return to the Modify Style dialog box. Click **OK** to return to the Styles dialog box and click **Close** to return to your document.

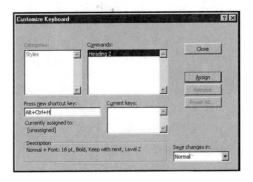

Figure 15.4   Assign shortcut keys to styles in the Customize Keyboard dialog box.

You can assign any function (F1–F12) key by itself, but this isn't a good idea because the function keys have Word commands already assigned to them. For example, you can assign the F1 key to a style, but then you will no longer be capable of accessing Help with F1. It is better to use key combinations. The following are available:

Ctrl+*key*

Alt+*key*

Ctrl+Alt+*key*

Ctrl+Shift+*key*

Alt+Shift+*key*

Ctrl+Alt+Shift+*key*

 Pre-assigned Key Combinations   Avoid assigning Ctrl+*key* and Alt+*key* combinations because many of these are already assigned to Word's menus and built-in commands.

FINDING AND REPLACING STYLES

It's easy enough to change the style of a single paragraph, but what about changing the style of dozens of paragraphs all through the document? For example, you might need to change all paragraphs that have the Normal style to a new style named Fancy1. Or, perhaps you simply need to locate paragraphs that have a particular style assigned. Word's Find and Replace command can help you. Following is how to find paragraphs formatted with a specific style:

1. Click **Edit, Find** or press **Ctrl+F** to open the Find tab of the Find and Replace dialog box.

2. Click **More** to display all the Find options.

3. Do not enter anything in the Find What text box. Instead, click the **Format** button, and then select **Style**.

4. The Find Style dialog box appears (see Figure 15.5). Select the style you want to find.

5. Click **OK** to return to the Find dialog box.

6. Click **Find Next** to begin the search.

Figure 15.5 You can use the Find Style dialog box to find and replace styles in your document.

The following steps show you how to find and replace a style:

1. Click **Edit, Replace** or press **Ctrl+H** to open the Replace tab of the Find and Replace dialog box.

2. Click **More** to display all the Replace options.

3. Click the **Find What** text box, but do not enter anything.

4. Click the **Format** button and select **Style** to open the Find Style dialog box (refer to Figure 15.5).

5. Select the style you want to replace, then click **OK** to return to the Find and Replace dialog box.

6. Click the **Replace With** text box, but again do not enter anything.

7. Click the **Format** button and select **Style** to open the Replace Style dialog box.

8. Select the replacement style, then click **OK** to return to the Find and Replace dialog box. The format selected is shown directly beneath the Find What and Replace With boxes.

9. To replace the style in individual paragraphs, click the **Find Next** and **Replace** buttons. To replace all instances of the first style with the second style, click the **Replace All** button.

After using the Find and Replace dialog box to work with styles, you have to remove the formats with the **No Formatting** button before you can find or replace plain text. Click in the **Find What** text box and click **No Formatting**. Then click in the **Replace With** text box and click **No Formatting**. If you don't remove the formats, Word thinks you are looking for text with that specific formatting when you do your next text find or replace.

In this lesson, you learned how to assign styles automatically, how to use the heading styles in Outline view, and how to specify spacing between paragraphs. You also learned how to assign shortcut keys to styles and how to find and replace styles. The next lesson, "Working with Margins, Pages, and Sections," shows you how to work with margins, pages, and sections.

LESSON 16

WORKING WITH MARGINS, PAGES, AND SECTIONS

In this lesson you learn how to use document sections, set page margins, work with different paper sizes, and specify the source of paper used in printing.

BREAKING A DOCUMENT INTO SECTIONS

Word gives you the option of breaking your document into two or more sections, each of which can have its own page formatting. You need to use document sections only when you want some aspect of page layout, such as page margins (covered later in this lesson) or columns (covered in Lesson 21, "Arranging Text into Columns"), to apply to only part of the document. The default is for page layout settings such as these to apply to the entire document—in other words, the entire document is treated as a single section.

There are three types of section breaks. They have the same effect in terms of controlling page layout, but differ as to where the text that comes after the break is placed:

- **Next Page**   The new section begins at the top of the next page. This is useful for section breaks that coincide with major breaks in a document, such as the beginning of a new chapter.

- **Continuous**   The new section begins on the same page as the preceding section. This is useful for a section that has a different number of columns from the preceding section but is still part of the same page. An example is a newsletter: The title runs across the top of the page in one column, and then, after a section break, the body of the newsletter appears below the title in three columns.

- **Odd Page or Even Page**   The new section begins on the next even- or odd-numbered page. This is useful when a section break coincides with a major break (such as a chapter) in a document where each chapter must start on an odd page (or an even page).

Can't Find the Section Breaks?   In Normal view, Word marks the location of section breaks by displaying a double horizontal line with the label Section Break, followed by the type of break. These markers do not appear in Print Layout view or in printouts.

To insert a section break at the insertion point:

1. Click **Insert, Break** to open the Break dialog box.

2. Select the desired type of section break (as described in the previous list).

3. Click **OK**.

A section break mark is just like any character in your document. To delete a section break, move the cursor right before it and press **Delete**, or move the cursor right after it and press **Backspace**.

Section Breaks Hold Page Layout Formatting   Each section break marker holds the settings for the text that comes before it. So, when you delete a section break, text in the section before the break becomes part of the section that was after the break and therefore assumes the page layout formatting of that section.

INSERTING MANUAL PAGE BREAKS

When text reaches the bottom margin of a page, Word automatically starts a new page and continues the text at the top of that page. However, you can manually insert page breaks to start a new page at any desired location. To insert a page break at the location of the insertion point:

1. Click **Insert, Break** to open the Break dialog box.

2. Select **Page Break**.

3. Click **OK**.

 Quick Breaks   You can enter a page break by pressing **Ctrl+Enter**. To start a new line without starting a new paragraph, press **Shift+Enter**.

A page break appears in the document as a single horizontal line. Like section break markers, page break markers do not appear in Print Layout view or in printouts. To delete a page break, click on the **Page Break** line and press **Delete**.

SETTING PAGE MARGINS

The page margins control the amount of white space between your text and the edges of the page. Each page has four margins: left, right, top, and bottom. When you change page margins, the new settings affect the entire document; or, if you have inserted one or more section breaks, the current section is affected.

The easiest way to set page margins is with your mouse and the ruler. You can work visually rather than thinking in terms of inches or centimeters. To display the ruler, click **View, Ruler** or position the mouse pointer near the top edge of the work area to temporarily display the ruler.

You can use the ruler to change margins only when working in Print Layout view (click **View** and then **Print Layout**). In Print Layout view, Word displays both a horizontal ruler at the top of the page and a vertical ruler on the left edge of the page. This permits you to set both the left/right and the top/bottom margins.

On each ruler, the white bar shows the current margin settings, as shown in Figure 16.1. To change the left or right margin, point at the margin marker on the horizontal ruler, at the left or right end of the white bar; the mouse pointer changes to a two-headed arrow. Then, drag the margin to the new position. For the top or bottom margin, follow the same procedure using the vertical ruler.

 Margins The margins are the distances between the text and the edges of the page.

Left margin line   Right margin line

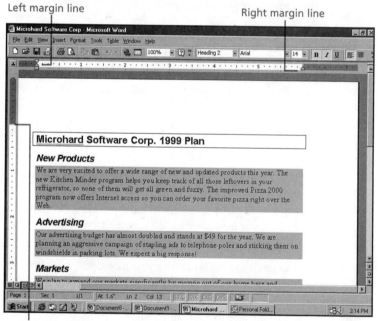

Top margin line

Figure 16.1 The ruler displays a white bar showing the current margin settings.

Note that the margin symbols on the horizontal ruler are the vertical edges of the white margin bar, not the small triangular buttons. These buttons are the indent markers, which you learned about in Lesson 11, "Applying Indents and Justification." If your mouse pointer has changed to a two-headed arrow, then you know you have found the margin symbol.

Changing Margins Margins apply to the entire section, unlike indents (which apply to individual paragraphs). To change the margins for only a portion of a document, insert one or more section breaks as described previously in this lesson. You can then specify different margins for each section.

Can't Change Margins? Be sure you're in Page Layout view or the rulers won't work for changing margins. (You can, however, drag the indent markers on the ruler in Normal view, as you learned in Lesson 11.)

You can also set the page margins using a dialog box. Use this method when you don't want to use the mouse or need to enter precise margin values. You also don't have to switch to Page Layout view to do it. It gives you more control over where in the document the new margins are applied. Here's how:

1. Click **File**, **Page Setup** to open the Page Setup dialog box.

2. If necessary, click the **Margins** tab to display the margins options, as shown in Figure 16.2.

3. In the **Top**, **Bottom**, **Left**, and **Right** text boxes, enter the desired margin size (in inches) or click the increment arrows to set the desired value. The Preview shows you the effects of your margin settings.

4. If your document will be bound and you want to leave an extra large margin on one side for the binding, enter the desired width in the **Gutter** text box. This extra space is added to the left margin of every page; or, if you select the **Mirror Margins** check box, it is added to the left margin of odd-numbered pages and the right margin of even-numbered pages (which is useful for binding a document that is printed on both sides of the paper).

5. Click the **Apply To** drop-down arrow and, from the list, select where you want the new margins to apply. Your options are as follows:

   - **Whole Document**   Apply the new margin settings to the entire document.

   - **This Point Forward**   Word inserts a continuous section break at the cursor location and applies the new margins to the new section.

   - **This Section**   Apply margins to the current document section. This option is not available if you have not broken your document into sections.

6. Click **OK**.

 Leave Room for Headers and Footers   Headers and footers are located within the top and bottom margins, respectively. A document with a header and footer might therefore need larger than normal margins.

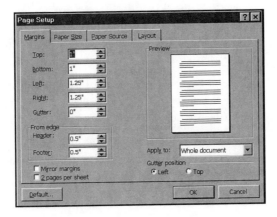

Figure 16.2   Set margins in the Page Setup dialog box.

CONTROLLING PAPER SIZE AND ORIENTATION

The default in Word is to format documents to fit on standard 8 1/2- by 11-inch paper, and to print in portrait orientation, which means the lines of text run parallel to the short edge of the paper. You can specify a different paper size, selecting from several standard paper and envelope sizes—or you can define a custom paper size. You can also print in landscape orientation, so the lines of text are parallel to the long edge of the paper.

To specify paper size and orientation:

1. Click **File**, **Page Setup** to open the Page Setup dialog box.

2. Click the **Paper Size** tab (see Figure 16.3).

3. Click the **Paper Size** drop-down arrow and select a predefined paper size from the list. Or, enter a custom height and width in the text boxes provided.

4. Select **Portrait** or **Landscape** orientation.

5. Click the **Apply To** drop-down arrow and select the portion of

the document to which the new paper setting will apply:

- **Whole Document**   Use the new paper setting for the entire document.

- **This Point Forward**   Word inserts a continuous section break at the cursor location and applies the new paper settings to the new section.

- **This Section**   Apply paper settings to the current document section. This option is not available if your document has not been broken into sections.

6. Select **OK**.

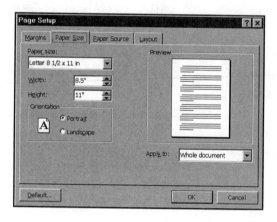

Figure 16.3   Set paper size and orientation in the Page Setup dialog box.

SPECIFYING A PAPER SOURCE

Some documents require printing on different kinds of paper. For example, with a multipage business letter you might want to print the first page on company letterhead and the other pages on plain paper. Within the limitations of your printer, you can tell Word where to get the paper for each section of the document. Most laser printers give you two choices: the regular paper tray or manual feed. Advanced printers have more options, such as two or more paper trays and an envelope feeder.

To specify the paper source:

1. Click **File**, **Page Setup** to open the Page Setup dialog box.

2. Click the **Paper Source** tab (see Figure 16.4).

3. In the **First Page** list box, specify the paper source for the first page. The choices available here depend on your printer model.

4. In the **Other Pages** list box, specify the paper source for the second and subsequent pages.

5. Click the **Apply To** drop-down arrow and select the part of the document to which you want the paper source settings to apply.

6. Select **OK**.

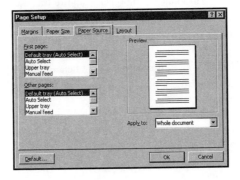

Figure 16.4   Specify the paper source in the Page Setup dialog box.

In this lesson you learned how to use document sections, how to set page margins, how to work with different paper sizes, and how to specify the source of paper used in printing. In the next lesson, "Adding Page Numbers, Headers, and Footers," you will learn how to add page numbers, headers, and footers to a document.

LESSON 17

ADDING PAGE NUMBERS, HEADERS, AND FOOTERS

In this lesson you learn how to add page numbers, headers, and footers to your documents.

ADDING PAGE NUMBERS

Many documents—particularly long ones—require that the pages be numbered. Although page numbers are always part of a header or footer, Word offers many choices as to their placement and appearance. You can place a page number by itself in a header or footer, as covered in this section. You can also include additional information in the header or footer, as covered later in this lesson. Use the following steps to add page numbers to your document.

 Headers and Footers Text that is displayed at the top (header) or bottom (footer) of every page.

1. Click **Insert, Page Numbers**. The Page Numbers dialog box appears (see Figure 17.1).

2. Click the **Position** drop-down arrow and select the desired position on the page: **Top of Page (Header)** or **Bottom of Page (Footer)**.

3. Click the **Alignment** drop-down arrow and select **Left**, **Center**, or **Right**. You can also select **Inside** or **Outside** if you're printing two-sided pages and want the page numbers positioned near to (inside) or away from (outside) the binding.

4. Turn off the **Show Number on First Page** option if you do not want a page number printed on the first page of the document (for example, a title page).

5. The default number format consists of Arabic numerals (1, 2, 3, and so on). To select a different format (such as i, ii, iii), click **Format** to display the Page Number Format dialog box.

6. Select the desired format in the Number Format drop-down list, then click **OK** to return to the Page Numbers dialog box.

7. Select **OK** to close the Page Numbers dialog box.

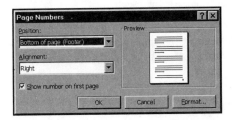

Figure 17.1 Use the Page Numbers dialog box to add page numbers to your document.

When you add a page number using this procedure, Word makes the page number part of the document's header or footer. If you already have a header or footer, the page number is added to it. The next section describes headers and footers.

No Page Numbers Command? When you're in Outline or Web Layout view, the Page Numbers option is not available on the Insert menu. In Normal view, you can add—but not see—page numbers.

WHAT ARE HEADERS AND FOOTERS?

A *header* or *footer* is text that prints at the top (header) or bottom (footer) of every page of a document. Headers and footers can show the page number and are useful for displaying chapter titles, authors' names, and similar information. Word offers several header/footer options, including the following:

- The same header/footer on every page of the document.

- One header/footer on the first page of the document and a different header/footer on all other pages.

- One header/footer on odd-numbered pages and a different header/footer on even-numbered pages.

- If your document is divided into sections, you can have a different header/footer for each section.

ADDING OR EDITING A HEADER OR FOOTER

To add a header or footer to your document, or to edit an existing header or footer, follow these steps:

1. If your document is divided into sections, move the cursor to any location in the section where you want the header or footer placed.

2. Click **View, Header and Footer**. Word switches to Print Layout view and displays the current page's header enclosed in a nonprinting dashed line (see Figure 17.2). Regular document text is dimmed, and the Header and Footer toolbar is displayed. On the toolbar, click the **Switch Between Header and Footer** button to switch between the current page's header and footer.

3. Enter the header or footer text and formatting using the normal Word editing techniques. Use the **Alignment** buttons on the Formatting toolbar to control the placement of items in the header/footer. Press **Tab** to move to the center and right parts of the header or footer. Press **Enter** to start a new line in the header or footer.

4. Use the other toolbar buttons (described in Table 17.1) to perform the indicated actions.

5. When finished, click the **Close** button on the Header and Footer
   toolbar to return to the document. To delete the contents of a
   header or footer, select all the text therein, and then press **Delete**.

Table 17.1   HEADER AND FOOTER TOOLBAR BUTTONS

BUTTON	DESCRIPTION
Insert AutoText ▾	Inserts an AutoText entry (see Lesson 18, "Saving Time with AutoCorrect and AutoText")
[#]	Inserts a page number code
[+]	Inserts the total number of pages
[#]	Formats the page number
[z]	Inserts a date code
[clock]	Inserts a time code
[book]	Opens the Page Setup dialog box so that you can set margins (see Lesson 16, "Working with Margins, Pages, and Sections")
[icon]	Shows or hides document text
[icon]	Switches between header and footer
[icon]	Shows the previous header or footer
[icon]	Shows the next header or footer

Document text is grayed.   Header and Footer toolbar   Header bar

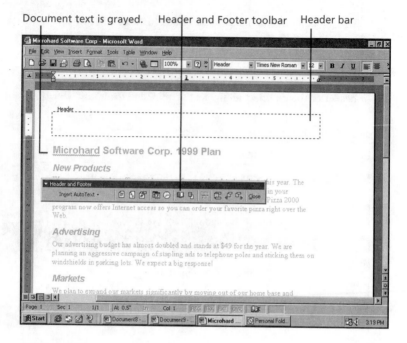

Figure 17.2 You use the Header and Footer toolbar to work with headers and footers.

CREATING DIFFERENT HEADERS AND FOOTERS FOR DIFFERENT PAGES

Word's default is to display the same header/footer on all the pages in a section or document. One way to have different headers/footers in different parts of the document is to break the document into two or more sections, as explained in Lesson 16. Then, you can use the techniques described earlier in this lesson to add a different header/footer to each section.

In addition to using sections, you have the following options:

- One header/footer on the first page with a different header/footer on all other pages.

- One header/footer on odd-numbered pages with another header/footer on even-numbered pages.

Use the following steps to activate one or both of these options:

1. Click **View, Header and Footer**.

2. Click the **Page Setup** button on the Header and Footer toolbar. Word displays the Layout tab of the Page Setup dialog box (see Figure 17.3).

3. Select the **Different Odd and Even** check box or the **Different First Page** check box.

4. Select **OK** to close the Page Setup dialog box.

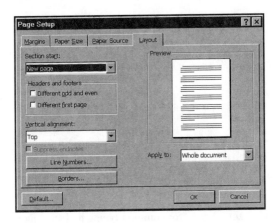

Figure 17.3 Set header/footer options in the Page Setup dialog box.

After selecting one of these header/footer options, use the techniques described earlier in this lesson to add and edit the header/footer text. For example, say you specified Different Odd and Even. If the cursor is on an even-numbered page, you can edit the header/footer text that displays on even-numbered pages. If you click the **Show Next** button on the Header/Footer toolbar, you move to the header/footer for odd-numbered pages.

In this lesson you learned to add page numbers, headers, and footers to a document. In the next lesson, "Saving Time with AutoCorrect and AutoText," you learn how to save time with AutoCorrect and AutoText.

LESSON 18

SAVING TIME WITH AUTOCORRECT AND AUTOTEXT

In this lesson you learn how to use Word's AutoCorrect and AutoText features to automatically correct errors and insert text.

WHAT DO AUTOCORRECT AND AUTOTEXT DO?

AutoCorrect and AutoText are very useful features that can save you a great deal of time. They're related to each other, but each one has a different purpose:

- **AutoCorrect** Looks for common typing and spelling mistakes in your document and automatically corrects them as they happen. For example, you can tell AutoCorrect to always replace *teh* with *the*.

- **AutoText** Enables you to define and store frequently used sections of text or graphics, and then insert them in the document as needed. For example, you can define an AutoText entry containing your complete name and address, and then insert it with a few keystrokes.

 Where's My Glossary? In previous versions of Word, the AutoText feature was called the Glossary.

DEFINING AN AUTOCORRECT ENTRY

There are two parts to AutoCorrect. One part deals with capitalization errors, such as forgetting to capitalize the first letter of a sentence. The other deals with spelling errors and the addition of special symbols. Thus, AutoCorrect can automatically replace *acn* with *can*, and it can replace "- >" with an arrow symbol. Word has a number of default AutoCorrect entries—but you can also create your own.

Text that AutoCorrect inserts can be plain text that takes on the paragraph formatting at the location where it is inserted, or it can be formatted text that retains its original formatting. The following steps show you how to create AutoCorrect entries:

1. If you want to create a formatted AutoCorrect entry, you must select the formatted text in the document. If you want the entry to be inserted as a separate paragraph, be sure to select the paragraph mark at the end of the text. To create a plain text AutoCorrect entry, selecting text is optional.

2. Click **Tools, AutoCorrect** to open the AutoCorrect dialog box (see Figure 18.1).

3. In the Replace box, type the text to be replaced. This is the text that will be replaced when you type it in the document (for example, *teh*).

4. If you selected document text in step 1, it will already be entered in the With text box. Otherwise, type the desired replacement text in the With text box (for example, *the*).

5. Select the **Formatted Text** option if you want the text's formatting to be inserted as well. Select the **Plain Text** option to insert the text without formatting.

6. Click the **Add** button. If the replacement text you specified is already defined in the AutoCorrect list, Word asks if you want to redefine it. If not, select **No** to return to step 3. Otherwise, select **Yes**.

7. Click **OK**.

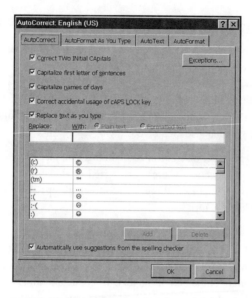

Figure 18.1 Defining an AutoCorrect entry in the AutoCorrect dialog box.

While you are editing a document, AutoCorrect checks complete words only. Thus, if you type *teh*, Word does not replace it with *the* until you press spacebar, period, or some other key indicating the end of the word.

Bad Speller? Define AutoCorrect entries for the words you commonly misspell and you won't have to spend time correcting them manually.

MODIFYING AUTOCORRECT SETTINGS

You can modify the AutoCorrect settings so it works the way you want. You might want to delete some of the many AutoCorrect entries that are predefined in Word. For example, if you work for a company named ACN Consulting you do not want the *ACN* corrected to *CAN* every time you type it. To modify AutoCorrect settings, follow these steps:

1. Click **Tools**, **AutoCorrect** to open the AutoCorrect dialog box (refer to Figure 18.1).

2. Do any of the following:

- To control the way AutoCorrect deals with capitalization errors, select or deselect the four check boxes at the top of the dialog box.

- To enable or disable automatic text replacement, select or deselect the **Replace Text as You Type** check box.

- To delete an individual AutoCorrect entry, select it in the list and click **Delete**.

- To modify an entry, select it in the list, edit the text in the With text box, and select **Replace**.

3. Click **OK**.

Word also enables you to customize the way that AutoCorrect's Correct Two Initial Capitals and Capitalize First Letter of Sentences features operate:

- Certain acronyms or other abbreviations might properly have two initial capitals; you can specify that AutoCorrect ignore them.

- Word capitalizes the first letter of a sentence based on the end of the previous sentence as marked by a period or other character. If, however, a sentence contains an abbreviation with a period (such as *acct.*), you do not want the next word capitalized. Word has a default list of abbreviations to be ignored; you can modify this list as needed.

Here's how to customize AutoCorrect's capitalization settings:

1. Click **Tools, AutoCorrect** to open the AutoCorrect dialog box.

2. Click the **Exceptions** button to open the AutoCorrect Exceptions dialog box.

3. Click the **INitial CAps** tab, then enter the acronym to be ignored in the Don't Correct text box and select **Add**. Select an acronym in the list and click **Delete** to remove it.

4. Click the **First Letter** tab and enter the abbreviation to be ignored in the Don't Capitalize After text box, then select **Add**. Select an abbreviation in the list and click **Delete** to remove it.

5. Select **OK** to return to the AutoCorrect dialog box.

Note that AutoCorrect works only on text you type. For example, if you open a document that was created by someone else, AutoCorrect does not correct errors in the document.

CREATING AUTOTEXT DEFINITIONS

Word enables you to store any text and graphics in a named AutoText entry. You can then insert the text or graphics in any document simply by typing or selecting its name.

When you create an AutoText entry, it is linked to the paragraph style of the original text from which the entry was created. When you need to insert an AutoText entry, the list displays only those entries associated with the paragraph style of the paragraph containing the cursor. The exception is when the cursor is in a paragraph with the Normal paragraph style, in which case all AutoText entries are available. Thus, if you create an AutoText entry from text in a paragraph formatted with a style named Formal, that AutoText entry is available only when the cursor is in a paragraph that has the style Formal or the style Normal applied to it.

 The AutoText Toolbar If you use AutoText frequently, you might find it convenient to have the AutoText toolbar displayed. Click **View, Toolbars, AutoText**.

To create an AutoText entry:

1. Select the text or graphics to be included in the entry. If you want the text's formatting included as part of the entry, be sure to include the paragraph marker in the selection.

2. Press **Alt+F3** or click **Insert, AutoText, New**. The Create
   AutoText dialog box appears (see Figure 18.2).

3. You can accept the AutoText name that Word suggests or enter
   your own in the box. This is the name that Word will use to
   identify the fact that you want to enter this AutoText.

4. Select **OK**.

 Tip If the AutoText toolbar is displayed, you can
define a new AutoText entry by clicking the **New**
button.

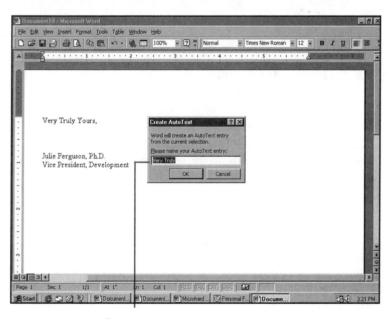

AutoText entry name

Figure 18.2   Use the Create AutoText dialog box to create a new
AutoText entry.

INSERTING AUTOTEXT

There are several methods available for inserting AutoText entries into your document at the insertion point:

- If the AutoText toolbar is displayed, click the middle button. This button is labeled with the name of the current paragraph style if that style has any AutoText entries associated with it. If the current style is Normal or has no associated AutoText entries, the button is labeled All Entries. Select the desired AutoText entry from the list.

- If AutoComplete is enabled (see the following steps), start typing the name of the AutoText entry. When you have typed enough of the name to identify the entry, Word displays the matching AutoText entry in a small tip box next to the cursor (as shown in Figure 18.3). To insert the entire entry, press **F3** or **Enter**. To ignore it, simply keep typing.

- Click **Insert, AutoText**. The next submenu displays the AutoText entries, if any, that are associated with the current paragraph, and you can select the desired entry. If the current paragraph style is Normal or has no associated AutoText entries, the submenu displays a list of styles that have AutoText entries associated with them. Select the style that has the entry you want, then select the desired entry.

If the current paragraph has been assigned a paragraph style other than Normal, and that style has one or more AutoText entries associated with it, the AutoText list displays only those entries that have been associated with that style. To display all AutoText entries in this situation, hold down the **Shift** key while clicking the **AutoText** toolbar or when selecting **AutoText** from the Insert menu.

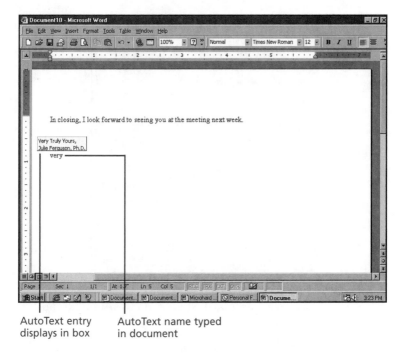

AutoText entry   AutoText name typed
displays in box   in document

Figure 18.3   Use AutoComplete to insert an AutoText entry.

The AutoComplete option is controlled from the AutoText tab of the
AutoCorrect dialog box. You also use this tab to delete AutoText entries.
Here are the steps to follow:

1. Click **Insert**, **AutoText**, then **AutoText** again, or click the button at the left end of the AutoText toolbar to open the AutoText
   dialog box (see Figure 18.4).

2. Select or deselect the **Show AutoComplete Tip for AutoText
   and Dates** check box.

3. To delete an AutoText entry, select it in the list and click
   Delete.

4. Select **OK**.

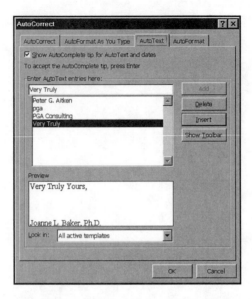

Figure 18.4   Selecting an AutoText entry on the AutoText tab of the AutoCorrect dialog box.

AUTOCORRECT VERSUS AUTOTEXT

You might have realized that you can use AutoCorrect to perform the task of AutoText, at least for inserting text. (AutoCorrect cannot insert graphics.) Thus, if your name is Heironymous J. Whipplesnapper, you can define an AutoCorrect entry *hjw* to automatically insert your name. The major difference is that AutoCorrect entries are inserted automatically, whereas AutoText entries require user confirmation. Note that every AutoText and AutoCorrect entry will be available in all documents you edit.

This lesson showed you how to use Word's AutoText and AutoCorrect features. The next lesson, "Using Symbols and Special Characters," shows you how to use international and special characters.

LESSON 19

USING SYMBOLS AND SPECIAL CHARACTERS

In this lesson you learn how to use symbols and special characters.

WHAT ARE SYMBOLS AND SPECIAL CHARACTERS?

Symbols and special characters are not part of the standard character set and, therefore, are not found on your keyboard. These include characters used in foreign languages, such as é and Ñ; symbols used in science and engineering, such as the Greek letters *mu* (μ) and *delta* (Δ); and special symbols such as copyright (©). Although these characters are not on your keyboard, Word can still insert them into your documents.

The distinction that Word makes between special characters and symbols is not a clear one. In fact, there is some overlap between the two. Symbols include letters with the accents and other diacritical marks used in some languages, Greek letters, arrows, and mathematical symbols (such as ±). Special characters include the copyright symbol (©), ellipses (…), and typographic symbols such as em spaces (a wider than normal space). You'll see that Word provides many more symbols than special characters.

INSERTING A SYMBOL

To insert a symbol in your document, follow these steps:

1. Click **Insert, Symbol** to open the Symbol dialog box (see Figure 19.1). Click the **Symbols** tab if it is not already displayed.

2. Click the **Font** drop-down arrow and select the desired symbol set from the list. The ones you will use most often are

   • Greek letters, mathematical symbols, arrows, trademark and copyright symbols, and so on.

   • Normal Text Letters with accents and other special marks, currency symbols, the paragraph symbol, and more.

   • WindDings Icons for clocks, envelopes, telephones, and so on.

3. Look through the grid of symbols for the one you want. To see an enlarged view of a symbol, click it.

4. To insert the highlighted symbol, select **Insert**. To insert any symbol, double-click it. The inserted symbol might be hidden from view by the dialog box.

5. Click the **Cancel** button to close the dialog box without inserting a symbol. Click **Close** to close the dialog box after you insert one or more symbols.

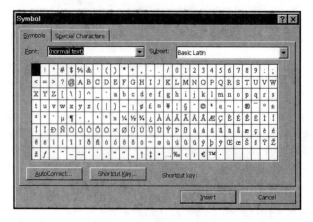

Figure 19.1 Use the Symbol dialog box to insert symbols in your document.

INSERTING A SPECIAL CHARACTER

To insert a special character in your document, use the following steps:

1. Click **Insert, Symbol** to open the Symbol dialog box.

2. Click the **Special Characters** tab to display the special characters list, as shown in Figure 19.2.

3. Look through the list of special characters for the one you want.

4. To insert a highlighted character, select **Insert**. To insert any character in the list, double-click it. The inserted character might be hidden from view by the dialog box.

5. Click the **Cancel** button to close the dialog box without inserting a character. Click **Close** to close the dialog box after you insert a character.

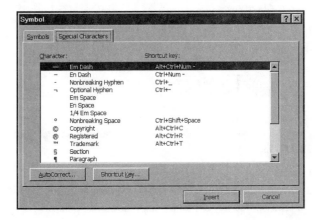

Figure 19.2   Insert a special character using the Special Characters list.

ASSIGNING SHORTCUT KEYS TO SYMBOLS

You might want to assign shortcut keys to symbols you use frequently. You can then insert a symbol quickly by pressing a specific key combination. Most of the special characters already have shortcut keys assigned to them; you can view these key assignments on the Special Character tab in the Symbol dialog box (refer to Figure 19.2).

More Shortcuts   You can also use Word's AutoCorrect feature to quickly insert symbols and special characters. See Lesson 18, "Saving Time with AutoCorrect and AutoText," for more information.

To assign a shortcut key to a symbol

1. Select **Insert**, **Symbol**, and then click the **Symbols** tab (refer to Figure 19.1).

2. Click the desired symbol. If necessary, first select the proper font from the Font list.

3. If the selected symbol already has a shortcut key assigned to it, the key description displays in the lower-right corner of the dialog box.

4. Click the **Shortcut Key** button to display the Customize Keyboard dialog box (see Figure 19.3).

5. Press **Alt+N** to move to the Press New Shortcut Key text box (or click in the box).

6. Press the shortcut key combination you want to assign. Its description appears in the Press New Shortcut Key text box. A list of permitted key combinations follows these steps.

   If the specified key combination is unassigned, Word displays [unassigned] under the Press New Shortcut Key text box. If it has already been assigned, Word displays the name of the symbol, macro, or command that the selected shortcut key is assigned to.

7. If the shortcut key is unassigned, click **Assign** to assign it to the symbol. If it is already assigned, press **Backspace** to delete the shortcut key display and return to step 6 to try another key combination.

8. When you are finished, select **Close** to return to the Symbols dialog box, and then select **Close** again to return to your document.

The shortcut keys are really key combinations; you can select from the following (where *key* is a letter key, number key, function key, or cursor movement key):

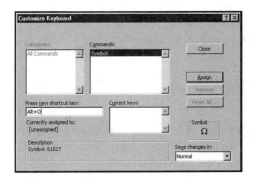

Figure 19.3   Assign a shortcut key to a symbol.

USES FOR SPECIAL CHARACTERS

Some of the special characters that Word offers might be unfamiliar to you, but they can be quite useful in certain documents. The following are brief descriptions of the less well-known characters:

• **En dash**   A dash that is slightly longer than the standard hyphen (inserted with the key above the P key on your keyboard). The en dash is properly used in combinations of figures and capital letters, as in, "Please refer to part 1–A."

- **Em dash**   Slightly longer than an en dash, the em dash has a variety of purposes; the most common use is to mark a sudden change of thought. For example, "She said—and no one dared disagree—that the meeting was over."

- **En space**   A space slightly longer than the standard space is an en space.

- **Em space**   A space slightly longer than the en space is an em space.

- **Non-breaking space**   A space that is not broken at the end of the line. The words separated by a non-breaking space always stay on the same line.

- **Non-breaking hyphen**   Similar to a non-breaking space. That is to say, two words separated by a non-breaking hyphen always stay on the same line.

- **Optional hyphen**   A hyphen that does not display unless the word it is in needs to be broken at the end of a line.

In this lesson you learned how to use symbols and special characters in your Word documents. In the next lesson, "Organizing Your Document with Tables," you will learn how use tables in your document.

LESSON 20

ORGANIZING YOUR DOCUMENT WITH TABLES

In this lesson you learn how to add tables to your document, and how to edit and format tables.

WHAT'S A TABLE?

A table enables you to organize information in a row and column format. Each entry, or *cell*, in a table is independent of all other entries. You can have almost any number of rows and columns in a table. You also have a great deal of control over the size and formatting of each cell. A table cell can contain text, graphics, and just about anything else that a Word document can contain. The one exception is that an inserted table cannot contain another table.

 On the Table   Use tables for columns of numbers, lists, and anything else that requires a row and column arrangement.

INSERTING A TABLE

To insert a new, empty table at any location within your document, follow these steps:

1. Move the cursor to the document location where you want the table.

2. Select **Table, Insert, Table**. The Insert Table dialog box appears (see Figure 20.1).

3. In the **Number of Columns** and **Number of Rows** text boxes, click the arrows or enter the number of rows and columns the table will have. You can change the number of columns and rows later.

4. To apply one of Word's automatic table formats to the table, click the **AutoFormat** button, select the desired format, and then click **OK**. (AutoFormat is covered in more detail later in this lesson.)

5. In the AutoFit Behavior section of the dialog box, select one of the following options for the width of columns in the table:

   - For equal column widths equally spaced across the page, select **Fixed Column Width** and select **Auto** in the adjacent box.

   - For equal column widths set at a specific size, select **Fixed Column Width,** and then the column width, in inches, in the adjacent box.

   - To have column widths automatically adjust to the table contents, select **AutoFit to Contents.** The new table has very narrow columns until you add text to the cells.

   - To have column widths automatically adjust to the screen width, select **AutoFit to Window.**

6. Select **OK.** A blank table is created with the cursor in the first cell.

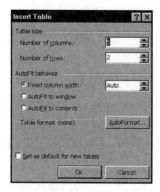

FIGURE 20.1 Use the Insert Table dialog box to create a table.

Quick Tables   To quickly insert a table, click the Insert Table button on the Standard toolbar, and then drag over the desired number of rows and columns.

WORKING IN A TABLE

When the cursor is in a table cell, you can enter and edit text as you do in the rest of the document. Text entered in a cell automatically wraps to the next line within the column width. You can move the cursor to any cell by clicking the cell. You can also navigate in a table using the following special key combinations:

Press this	To move here
Tab	The next cell in a row
Shift+Tab	The previous cell in a row
Alt+Home	The first cell in the current row
Alt+Page Up	The top cell in the current column
Alt+End	The last cell in the current row
Alt+Page Down	The last cell in the current column

If the cursor is at the edge of a cell, you can use the arrow keys to move between cells. To insert a tab in a table cell, press Ctrl+Tab.

EDITING AND FORMATTING A TABLE

After you create a table and enter some information, you can edit its contents and format its appearance to suit your needs.

DELETING AND INSERTING CELLS, ROWS, AND COLUMNS

You can clear individual cells in a table, erasing their contents and leaving a blank cell. You can also remove entire rows and columns. When you do so, columns to the right or rows below move to fill in for the deleted row or column.

Fast Select!   You can either select the text in the cell or the entire cell. To select an entire cell, click in the left margin of the cell, between the text and the cell border. The mouse pointer changes to an arrow when it's in this area.

To clear the contents of a cell, select the cell and press **Delete**.

To remove an entire row or column from the table, or to delete the entire table, use the following steps:

1. Move the cursor to any cell in the row or column to be deleted. To delete the entire table the cursor can be in any cell.

2. Click **Table**, **Delete**, and then from the submenu click one of the following:

   Table   Delete the entire table.

   Columns Delete the current column.

   Rows   Delete the current row.

You can also delete single cells (not just their contents) and have data in the same row or column move to fill in the space. To do this

1. Move the cursor to the cell you want to delete.

2. Click **Table**, **Delete**, **Cells** to display the Delete Cells dialog box (see Figure 20.2).

3. In this dialog box make one of the following choices:

   Select **Shift Cells Left** to have cells in the same row as the deleted cell shift left to fill in.

   Select **Shift Cells Up** to have cells in the same column as the deleted cell shift up to fill in.

4. Click **OK**.

Recovery   Remember that you can undo table editing actions by selecting **Edit, Undo**.

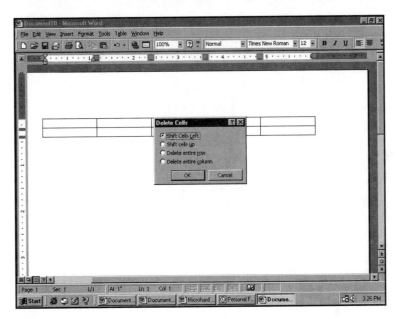

FIGURE 20.2   You use the Delete Cells dialog box to delete cells in
a table.

To insert a single row or column into a table

1. Move the cursor to a cell where you want the new column or
   new row.

2. Click **Table, Insert**, and from the submenu choose from the following selections:

   Columns to the Left   To add a new column to the left of the cursor location.

   Columns to the Right   To add a new column to the right of the
   cursor location.

Rows Above   To add a new row above the cursor location.

Rows Below   To add a new row below the cursor location.

To insert more than one row or column into a table:

1. Select cells that span the number of rows or columns you want to insert. For example, to insert three new rows between rows 2 and 3, select cells in rows 3, 4, and 5 (in any column).

2. Click **Table, Insert**.

3. From the submenu select the desired placement of the new rows or columns.

 Add a Row to the Bottom   To insert a new row at the bottom of the table, move the cursor to the last cell in the table and press **Tab**.

To insert a new column at the right edge of the table

1. Click any cell in the last row of the table.

2. Click **Table, Insert**.

3. From the submenu choose **Columns to the Right**.

Moving or Copying Columns and Rows

Here's how to copy or move an entire column or row from one location in a table to another:

1. Select the column or row by dragging over the cells or by clicking in the column or row. Next, click **Table, Select, Row**; or, you can click **Table, Select, Column**.

2. To copy, press **Ctrl+C** or click the **Copy** button on the Standard toolbar. To move, press **Ctrl+X** or click the **Cut** button.

3. Move the cursor to the new location for the column or row. It will be inserted above or to the left of the cursor location.

4. Press **Ctrl+V** or click the **Paste** button on the Standard toolbar.

Quick Mouse Moves   To quickly move table columns, rows, or cells with the mouse, select them and drag to the new location. To copy instead of moving, press and hold Ctrl while dragging.

CHANGING COLUMN WIDTH

You can quickly change the width of a column with the mouse:

1. Point at the right border of the column whose width you want to change. The mouse pointer changes to a pair of thin vertical lines with arrowheads pointing left and right.

2. Drag the column border to the desired width. The column to the right adjusts so that the overall table width remains the same.

You can also use a dialog box to change column widths:

1. Move the cursor to any cell in the column that you want to change.

2. Click **Table, Table Properties** to display the Table Properties dialog box. Click the **Column** tab if required (see Figure 20.3).

3. Be sure the **Preferred Width** option is selected. Then, from the Measure In list, select one of the following:

    - **Inches**   To specify the column width in inches.

    - **Percent**   To specify the column width as a percent of the total table width.

4. In the Preferred Width box enter the value, or click the increment arrows, to specify the inches or percent value for the column.

5. Click **Next Column** or **Previous Column** to change the settings for other columns in the table.

6. Select **OK**. The table changes to reflect the new column settings.

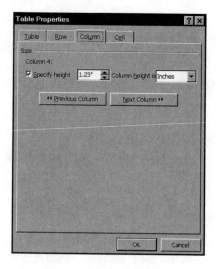

FIGURE 20.3   Use the Table Properties dialog box to change a table's column width.

ADDING BORDERS TO A TABLE

Word's default is to place a single, thin border around each cell in a table. You can modify the borders or remove them altogether. The techniques for working with table borders are essentially the same as for adding borders to other text (see Lesson 10, "Changing the Appearance of Text"). Briefly, here are the steps involved:

1. Select the table cells whose borders you want to modify.

2. Select **Format, Borders and Shading** to display the Borders and Shading dialog box. Click the **Borders** tab if necessary (see Figure 20.4).

3. Select the desired border settings, using the Preview box to see how your settings will appear.

4. Click **OK**.

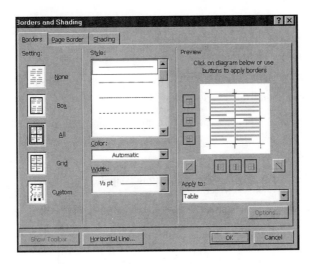

Figure 20.4   Use the Borders tab to modify table borders.

In a table with no borders, you can display non-printing gridlines
onscreen to make it easier to work with the table. Select **Table, Show
Gridline** to display gridlines, and select **Table, Hide Gridlines** to turn
them off.

AUTOMATIC TABLE FORMATTING

Word provides a variety of predefined table formats. Using these formats
makes it easy to apply attractive formatting to any table:

1. Place the cursor anywhere in the table.

2. Select **Table, Table AutoFormat**. The Table AutoFormat dialog
   box appears (see Figure 20.5). This is the same dialog box you
   see if you select **AutoFormat** in the Insert Table dialog box
   when first creating a table, as covered earlier in this lesson.

3. In the Formats list select from the available table formats. As you scroll through the list, the Preview box shows the appearance of the highlighted format.

4. Select and deselect the **Formats to Apply** check boxes as needed until the Preview shows the table appearance you want.

5. To control whether special formatting is applied to certain parts of the table, select and deselect options in the Apply Special Format To section.

6. Select **OK**. The selected formatting is applied to the table.

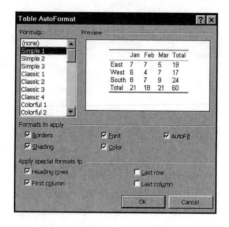

FIGURE 20.5   You can assign predefined table formats in the Table AutoFormat dialog box.

In this lesson you learned how to add tables to your document, and how to edit and format tables. The next lesson, "Arranging Text into Columns," shows you how to use columns in your documents.

LESSON 21

ARRANGING TEXT INTO COLUMNS

In this lesson you'll learn how to use columns in your document.

WHY USE COLUMNS?

Columns are commonly used in newsletters, brochures, and similar documents. The shorter lines of text provided by columns are easier to read, and they provide greater flexibility in formatting a document with graphics, tables, and other elements. Word makes it easy to use columns in your documents. Figure 21.1 shows a document formatted with three columns.

The columns that you create in Word are newspaper-style columns, which means that the text flows to the bottom of one column and then continues at the top of the next column on the page. For side-by-side paragraphs, such as those used in a resume or a script, use Word's table feature (as discussed in Lesson 20, "Organizing Your Document with Tables").

When you select text before defining columns, the column definition applies to the selected text. Word inserts section breaks before and after the selection. If you do not select text first the column definitions will apply to the entire document—unless you have divided the document into two or more sections, in which case the columns will apply only to the current section. See Lesson 16, "Working with Margins, Pages, and Sections," for more information about document sections.

FIGURE 21.1   Text formatted in columns wraps from the bottom of one column to the top of the next.

CREATING COLUMNS

Word has four predefined column layouts:

- Two equal width columns

- Three equal width columns

- Two unequal width columns with the narrower column on the left

- Two unequal width columns with the narrower column on the right

You can apply any of these column formats to an entire document, to one section of a document, to selected text, or from the insertion point onward. Follow these steps:

1. If you want only a part of the document in columns, select the text that you want in columns, or move the insertion point to the

location where you want columns to begin. Word inserts section breaks before and after the text as needed.

2. Select **Format, Columns** to open the Columns dialog box (see Figure 21.2).

3. Under **Presets**, click the column format you want.

4. Click the **Apply To** drop-down arrow and specify the extent to which the columns will apply. The following options are available:

   • **Whole Document**   This option is available only if the document has not been broken into sections.

   • **This Section**   This option is available only if you have broken the document into sections.

   • **Selected Text**   This option is available only if you selected text before opening the dialog box.

   • **This Point Forward**   Word inserts a section break at the current cursor location and applies the new column setting to the latter of the two sections.

5. Select the **Line Between** check box to display a vertical line between columns.

6. Select **OK**.

Word automatically switches to Print Layout view when you define columns because this is the only view that displays columns formatted properly on-screen.

Quick Columns   To display selected text, the current section, or the entire document in one to seven equal width columns, click the **Columns** button on the Standard toolbar, and then drag over the desired number of columns.

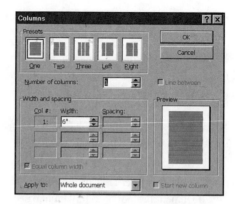

FIGURE 21.2   Use the Columns dialog box to format text in columns.

 No Columns? Columns display onscreen only in Print Layout view. In Normal view, Word displays only a single column at a time—but your multiple columns will look fine when printed, even from Normal view. To switch to Print Layout view, select **View, Print Layout.**

MODIFYING COLUMNS

You can modify existing columns, change the number of columns, change column widths, and change the spacing between columns. Use the following steps:

1. Move the insertion point to any location in the columns that you want to modify.

2. Select **Format, Columns** to open the Columns dialog box (refer to Figure 21.2). The options in the dialog box reflect the current settings for the columns you selected.

3. To apply a different predefined column format, click the desired format in the **Presets** area of the dialog box.

4. To change the width or spacing of a specific column, enter the desired width and spacing values—or click the arrows—in the

column's **Width and Spacing** text boxes. The Preview box shows you how the settings will look.

5. For equal width columns, select the **Equal Column Width** option, then specify the width and spacing for all columns under Col #1. For unequal width columns turn off the **Equal Column Width** option, and then specify the width and spacing for each column individually.

6. Select **OK**.

TURNING COLUMNS OFF

To convert multiple column text back to normal text (which is really just one column), follow these steps:

1. Move the insertion point to any location in the text that you want to change from multiple columns to a single column.

2. Select **Format, Columns** to open the Columns dialog box (refer to Figure 21.2).

3. Under **Presets**, select the **One** option.

4. Select **OK**.

 A Quicker Way   To quickly convert text in columns back to normal single-column text, put the insertion point in the text, click the **Columns** button on the Standard toolbar, and drag to select a single column.

This lesson showed you how to arrange text in columns. The next lesson, "Adding Graphics to Your Document," shows you how to work with graphics in your document.

LESSON 22

ADDING GRAPHICS TO YOUR DOCUMENT

In this lesson you learn how to add graphics to your documents and how to create your own drawings.

ADDING A GRAPHIC IMAGE

A *graphic image* is a picture that is stored on disk in a graphics file. Word can utilize images created by a variety of graphics applications, including Photoshop and PowerPoint, and a library of clip art images that you can use in your documents. Figure 22.1 shows a document with a graphic image.

To add a graphic image to a Word document, follow these steps:

1. Move the insertion point to the location for the graphic.

2. Select **Insert, Picture, From File**. The Insert Picture dialog box appears (see Figure 22.2).

3. If necessary, click the **Look In** drop-down arrow, or click one of the folder icons at the left of the dialog box, to specify the folder in which the graphic file is located.

FIGURE 22.1 You can insert graphics in your documents.

4. The list in the center of the dialog box normally lists all graphics files in the specified directory. To have the list restricted to certain types of graphics files, click the **Files of Type** drop-down arrow and select the desired file type from the list.

5. In the **File Name** text box, type the name of the file to insert or select the file name from the list. The image is previewed on the right side of the dialog box. If the image does not preview, click **View, Preview**.

6. Select **Insert**. The graphic is inserted into your document on top of the text, ready to be positioned.

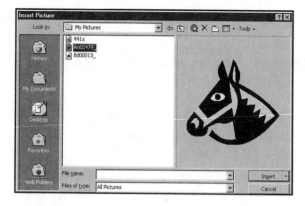

FIGURE 22.2   Use the Insert Picture dialog box to add a graphic to your document.

ADDING CLIP ART

Clip art is a special category of pictures that consists of generally small, simple images that you can use to add visual appeal and interest to your documents. Word comes with an extensive gallery of clip art that you can use freely. The following steps explain how to add a clip art image to a document:

1. Move the cursor to the document location where you want the image.

2. Select **Insert, Picture, Clip Art** to open the Insert ClipArt dialog box (see Figure 22.3). Be sure that the **Pictures** tab is selected.

3. In the dialog box, click on the icon of the category of pictures from which you want to select. The dialog box displays the clip

art images in that category. If you have Internet access, you can click the **Clips Online** button in the Insert ClipArt dialog box. This connects you to Microsoft's Web site, where you can access additional clip art images.

4. Scroll through the image list until you find the image you want. Or, click the **Back** button (the left-pointing arrow) at the top of the dialog box to return to the category list.

5. Click the desired image to display a pop-up menu (Figure 22.4).

6. Click the top icon on this menu to insert the clip in the document. The dialog box remains open.

7. Repeat steps 3 through 6 if you want to add more clip art images to the document.

8. When you are finished, close the dialog box by clicking the **X** at the right end of the title bar.

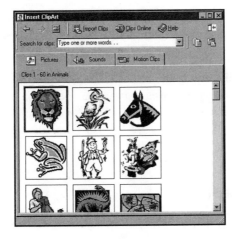

FIGURE 22.3   You can select clip art from the Insert ClipArt dialog box.

Click here to insert the clip ⎯

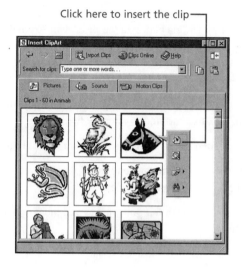

FIGURE 22.4   Use this pop-up menu to insert a selected clip.

CONTROLLING THE SCREEN DISPLAY OF GRAPHICS

The screen display of graphics images can slow down screen scrolling. If you're working on the document text and don't need to see the images, you can speed up screen display by displaying empty rectangles called *placeholders* in place of the images. You can control the display of graphics as follows:

1. Select **Tools, Options** to open the Options dialog box.

2. If necessary, click the **View** tab to display the View options.

3. In the Show section, select or deselect the **Picture Placeholders** check box.

4. Select **OK**.

The screen display of placeholders does not affect printing, which always includes the actual graphics.

Quick Graphics View   When using placeholders, you can get a quick view of the graphics by using Print Preview.

CROPPING AND RESIZING A GRAPHIC

You can change the size of images in your document; you can also crop them to display only part of the image. Before you can work with a graphic in your document, you must select it by clicking it with the mouse. A selected graphic is surrounded by eight small squares called sizing handles.

You can resize a graphic in your document, displaying the entire picture at a different size. You cannot, however, resize graphics when placeholders are displayed. You can resize a graphic and keep the original proportions—height to width ratio—or you can resize and change the proportions. Use the following steps to resize a graphic:

1. Select the graphic.

2. Point at one of the sizing handles (the mouse pointer will change to a double-headed arrow) as follows:

   • To resize and keep the original proportions, point at a sizing handle at one of the image's corners.

   • To resize and change the image proportions, point at a sizing handle in the middle of one of the image's edges.

3. Press the left mouse button and drag the handle until the outline of the graphic is the desired size. You can either enlarge or shrink the graphic.

4. Release the mouse button.

Whoops!   If you make a mistake when resizing or cropping a graphic, you can recover by selecting **Edit**, **Undo**.

DELETING, MOVING, AND COPYING GRAPHICS

To delete a graphic, select it and press **Delete**. To move or copy a graphic to a new location, do the following:

1. Select the graphic.

2. To copy the graphic, select **Edit, Copy** or press **Ctrl+C**. To move the graphic, select **Edit, Cut** or press **Ctrl+X**.

3. Move the cursor to the new location for the graphic.

4. Select **Edit, Paste** or press **Ctrl+V**.

 Shortcut Commands   Look to the Standard toolbar for Copy, Cut, and Paste buttons.

 Drag That Image   If the image and its destination are both in view, you can move it by dragging it to the new location. To copy instead of moving, hold down **Ctrl** while dragging.

DRAWING IN YOUR DOCUMENT

In addition to adding existing graphics to a document, Word enables you to create your own drawings. The drawing tools that are available enable even the complete non-artist to create professional-looking drawings. To draw, you must display the Drawing toolbar. To do so, select **View, Toolbars, Drawing**. Figure 22.5 shows the Drawing toolbar and identifies its buttons.

The process of drawing consists of the following general actions:

- **Adding drawing objects to the document**   The available objects include lines, arrows, shapes, and text. Most of Word's drawing objects are called AutoShapes.

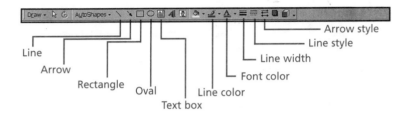

Line

Arrow

Rectangle   Oval

Text box

Line color

Font color

Line width

Line style

Arrow style

FIGURE 22.5   The Drawing toolbar provides tools that you can use to draw in your document.

- **Moving drawing objects**   You can move drawing objects to new locations and change their sizes and proportions.

- **Modifying drawing objects**   For example, you might change the thickness of a line, the color of text, or the type of arrowhead on an arrow.

The Drawing toolbar displays buttons for the most commonly needed drawing objects: lines, arrows, 3D shapes, and so on. You access the less common drawing objects via menus or dialog boxes associated with the Drawing toolbar. The following list explains the most frequently used drawing procedures:

- To draw an object, click its button on the Drawing toolbar, or click the **AutoShapes** button and select the shape from the list. To insert the object, draw in the document. The mouse pointer displays as a cross-hair while you are drawing. Hold down **Shift** while drawing to draw an object with a 1:1 aspect ratio (for example, a square or circle instead of a rectangle or ellipse).

Change Your Mind?   If you select a tool from the drawing toolbar and then change your mind about drawing, press **Esc** to cancel drawing.

- To select an object you have already drawn, click it. The object displays sizing handles. To select more than one object, hold down **Shift** while clicking. Press **Delete** to delete the selected object(s).

- To move a selected object, point at it (but not at a handle) and hold the left mouse button down while you drag it to the new location.

- To change a selected object's size or shape, point at one of its resizing handles and hold the left mouse button down while you drag it to the desired size/shape.

- To change the color of an object's line, click the **Line Color** button on the Drawing toolbar and select the desired color.

- To change the interior color of a solid object, click the **Fill Color** button and select the desired color.

- To change the thickness or style of the lines used for an object, select the object then click the **Line Style** or **Dash Style** button.

- To add a text label, click the **Text Box** button, drag in the document to add the text box, and then type the text. Click outside the text box when you finish.

Word's drawing capabilities go much further than what is described here. Experiment on your own to discover their full potential.

In this lesson you learned how to add graphics and drawings to your documents. The next lesson, "Working with Multiple Documents Simultaneously," teaches you how to work with multiple documents.

LESSON 23

WORKING WITH MULTIPLE DOCUMENTS SIMULTANEOUSLY

This lesson shows you how to simultaneously edit multiple documents in Word.

MULTIPLE DOCUMENTS?

Working on one document at a time is often all you need, but in some situations the capability to work on multiple documents at the same time can be very useful. For example, you can refer to one document while working on another, and you can copy and move text between documents. Word allows you to have as many documents as you need open simultaneously.

STARTING OR OPENING A SECOND DOCUMENT

While you're working on one document, you can start a new document or open another existing document at any time. To create a new document, follow the procedures you learned in Lesson 2, "Creating a New Document," and to open a document, refer to Lesson 4, "Saving and Opening Documents." Following is a brief list of options:

- To create a new document based on the Normal template, click the **New** button on the Standard toolbar.

- To create a document based on another template or on one of Word's Wizards, select **File, New**.

- To open an existing document, select **File, Open**, or click the **Open** button on the Standard toolbar.

A new program window opens and displays a new blank document or the document you opened. The document you were originally working on remains displayed in its own window, although it might be hidden by the new window. Both the newly opened document and the document you were working on are in memory and can be edited, printed, and so on. You can continue opening additional documents until all the files you need to work with are open.

 Opening Multiple Documents at Once   In the Open dialog box, you can select multiple documents by holding **Shift** while clicking the document names. Then, select **Open** to open all the selected documents, each in its own window.

SWITCHING BETWEEN DOCUMENTS

When you have multiple documents open at one time, only one of them can be active at a given moment. The active document is the only document displayed on-screen when the document window is maximized. If you have multiple windows displayed onscreen, the title bar of the active document is displayed in a darker color; if documents are overlapping each other, the active one will be on top. More importantly, the active document is the only one affected by editing commands.

Use the following steps to switch between open documents:

1. Select the **Window** menu. At the bottom is a list of all open documents, and there is a check mark next to the name of the currently active document (see Figure 23.1).

2. Select the name of the document that you want to be active. You can either click the document name with the mouse or press the corresponding number key.

The selected document becomes active and appears onscreen.

> **Next Please!**   To cycle to the next open document, press Ctrl+F6. You can also switch to any open document by clicking its icon in the Windows task bar.

Select from open documents

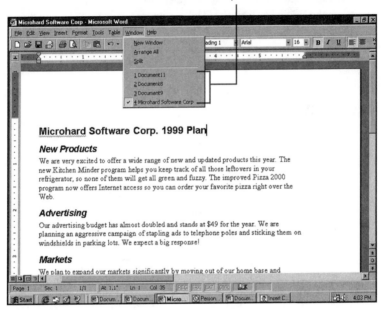

FIGURE 23.1   The Window menu lists open documents and indicates the currently active document.

CONTROLLING MULTIPLE DOCUMENT VIEW

Word gives you a great deal of flexibility in displaying multiple documents. You can have the active document occupy the entire screen, with other open documents temporarily hidden. You can also have several documents displayed at the same time, each in its own window. A document window can be in one of three states:

- **Maximized** The window occupies the entire screen and no other open documents are visible. Figure 23.1 shows a maximized document.

- **Minimized** The window is reduced to a small icon displayed on the Windows Task Bar. The document title is displayed on the icon. Note that Word's *W* symbol is also displayed on the Task Bar icon so you can distinguish document icons from those belonging to other programs.

- **Restored** The document window assumes an intermediate size, occupying part of your screen.

When multiple documents are open you can control their display as follows:

- To restore or minimize a maximized window, click its **Restore** or **Minimize** button.

- To maximize or minimize a restored window, click its **Maximize** or **Minimize** button.

- To display a minimized window, click its icon in the Task Bar.

 Watch Those Buttons!   The same location on Word's title bar is used to display the Maximize button when the document is restored, and the Restore button when the document is maximized.

When a document is in the restored state, you can control the size and position of its window on your screen. To move the window, point at its title bar and drag it to the new position. To change window size, point at a border or corner of the window (the mouse pointer changes to a two-headed arrow), and then press the left mouse button and drag the window to the desired size.

Viewing All Open Documents

Word has a command that displays all your open documents. Select **Window, Arrange All** to tile all document windows. When you tile your documents, every open document is displayed in a small window with no overlapping of windows. Each window has its own title bar, menu bar, and toolbars. If you have more than a few documents open, these windows will be quite small and won't be very useful for editing. They are useful, however, for seeing exactly what documents you have open and for finding the one you need to work on at the moment. Figure 23.2 shows the result of the Window, Arrange All command with three documents open.

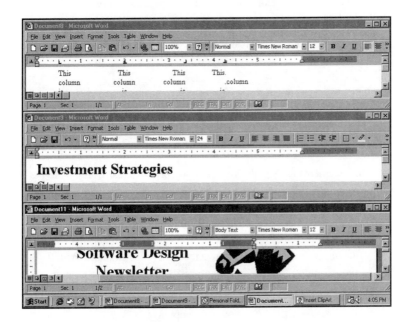

FIGURE **23.2** The Arrange All command displays all open documents, each in its own window.

MOVING AND COPYING TEXT BETWEEN DOCUMENTS

When you have more than one document open, you can move and copy text and graphics between documents. To do so, use the following procedure:

1. Make the source document active and select the text or graphic that is to be moved or copied.

2. If you want to move the text, click **Edit**, **Cut** or press **Ctrl+X**. If you want to copy the text, click **Edit**, **Copy** or press **Ctrl+C**.

3. Make the destination document active. Move the insertion point to the location for the text.

4. Click **Edit**, **Paste** or press **Ctrl+V**.

Use Your Toolbar   Remember that you can click the corresponding buttons on the standard toolbar to cut, copy, and paste.

If both documents are visible, you can copy or move text from one to the other with drag-and-drop:

1. Select the text to be copied or moved.

2. Point at the selected text with the mouse. The mouse changes from an I-beam to an arrow. To move the text, press and hold the left mouse button. To copy the text, press **Ctrl+left mouse button**.

3. Drag to the new location for the text and release the mouse button (and the Ctrl key, if you were copying).

No Arrow?   If your I-beam doesn't turn into an arrow when hovered over the selected text, you might have drag and drop editing turned off. Turn it on by clicking **Tools**, **Options**. On the **Edit** tab, select **Drag and Drop Text Editing**.

SAVING MULTIPLE DOCUMENTS

When you're working with multiple documents, you save an individual document (as you learned in Lesson 4) by selecting **File** from the menu of the document you want to save, and then choosing either **Save** or **Save As**. To save all open documents in one step, hold down **Shift** while selecting **File**; **Save** then becomes **Save All**. If you attempt to close a document that has not been saved, you are prompted to save it. If you try to quit Word with one or more unsaved documents, you are prompted to save each document, one by one.

CLOSING A DOCUMENT

You can close an open document when you finish working with it:

1. Make the document active.

2. Select **File, Close** or click the **Close** button at the right end of the document's title bar.

3. If the document contains unsaved changes, Word prompts you to save the document.

The document is closed.

 Close All   To close all documents at once, hold down **Shift** while selecting **File; Close** then becomes **Close All**.

This lesson showed you how to simultaneously edit multiple documents in Word. In the next lesson, "Creating and Modifying Document Templates," you will learn how to work with document templates.

LESSON 24

CREATING AND MODIFYING DOCUMENT TEMPLATES

In this lesson you learn how to create new document templates and how to modify existing templates.

CREATING A NEW TEMPLATE

You learned in Lesson 4, "Saving and Opening Documents," that every Word document is based on a template which contains formatting specifications and—optionally—text that will be part of the document. Word comes with a variety of predefined templates. You can also create your own templates, or modify existing templates, to suit your individual needs.

You can create a new template based on an existing template, and the new template will contain all the elements of the base template plus any text or formatting you add. To create a new template from scratch, base it on the Blank Document template. Here are the steps to follow:

1. Select **File, New** to open the New dialog box (see Figure 24.1).

2. Under Create New, click the **Template** option button.

3. If you want the new template to be based on an existing template, select that template's icon in the dialog box. Otherwise, select the **Blank Document** icon.

4. Select **OK**. A blank document editing screen appears with a default name, such as TEMPLATE1.

5. Enter the boilerplate text and other items, such as a header or footer, that you want to be part of the new template; apply formatting to the text as desired. You also need to create or modify any styles that you want in your new template.

6. Select **File, Save** or click the **Save** button on the Standard toolbar. The Save As dialog box appears.

7. Word's default is to save templates in the Template folder. Do not save templates in any other folder—if you do they will not be available in the New dialog box.

8. In the **File Name** text box, enter a descriptive name up to 256 characters long for the template. Be sure to use a different name from the template that you selected in step 3, or the new template will replace the original one.

9. Select **Save**. The template is saved under the specified name and is now available for use each time you start a new document.

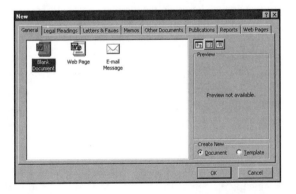

FIGURE 24.1 Create a new template based on the Blank Document template.

 Boilerplate   The text that you want to appear in every document based on the new template.

Modifying an Existing Template

You can retrieve any existing template from disk and modify it:

1. Select **File, New** to open the New dialog box.

2. Select the tab containing the template you want to modify, and then select the template icon you want to modify.

3. Under Create New, select the **Template** option button.

4. Click **OK**. The template is opened and displayed for editing.

5. Make the desired modifications and additions to the template's text and styles.

6. Select **File, Save** or click the **Save** button on the Standard toolbar. The modified template is saved to disk using its original name.

When you modify a template, changes you make are not reflected in documents that were created based on the template before it was changed. Only new documents will be affected.

 Save the Old   Rather than modifying a template, it's often better to create a new template based on it. This way the original template is still available if you change your mind.

 Recycle Old Templates?   You can use old templates from earlier versions of Word (for Windows 95 and for Windows 97) to create new documents in Word.

CREATING A TEMPLATE FROM A DOCUMENT

Sometimes you might find it useful to create a template based on an existing Word document. Here are the steps to follow:

1. Open the document that you want to use as the basis for the new template.

2. Use Word's editing commands to delete any document text and formatting that you do not want to appear in the template.

3. Select **File, Save As** to open the Save As dialog box (see Figure 24.2).

4. Click the **Save as Type** drop-down arrow and choose **Document Template** from the list. The Save In box automatically changes to indicate the Templates folder.

5. Type a descriptive name for template in the **File Name** text box.

6. Select **Save**.

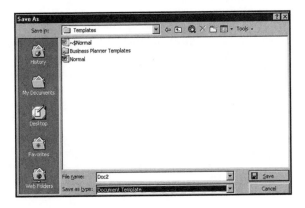

FIGURE 24.2   Saving a document template.

UPDATING A DOCUMENT WHEN THE TEMPLATE CHANGES

If you modify a template, only new documents based on that template will reflect the changes. Existing documents that were based on the old version of the template will not be affected. You can, however, import new styles from a modified template to an existing document. Use the following steps to do so:

1. Open the document.

2. Select **Tools, Templates and Add-ins**.

3. Select the **Automatically Update Document Styles** check box.

4. Select **OK**.

With this check box selected, the document styles are automatically updated to reflect the styles in its attached template each time the document is loaded. If the template has been modified, the changes are reflected in the document. Other elements of a template, such as boilerplate text, are not affected.

In this lesson you learned how to create and modify document templates. The next lesson, "Word and the World Wide Web," shows you how to use Word with the World Wide Web.

LESSON 25

WORD AND THE WORLD WIDE WEB

In this lesson you learn you how to use Word in conjunction with the World Wide Web.

WHAT IS THE WEB?

The *World Wide Web*, or *Web* for short, is part of the *Internet*, a world-wide network that enables computer users to share information and resources. The Web uses a specific document format called *hypertext markup language* (*HTML*) for its information. The Web also uses a type of address called a *uniform resource locator*, or *URL*, to identify specific documents and locations. Word offers a number of capabilities to help you work with HTML documents and URLs.

 HTML Acronym for hypertext markup language, the document format used on the Web.

CREATING A WEB DOCUMENT

You can save any Word document in HTML format, which permits it to be used on the Web. You create and edit the document using the usual Word techniques, arranging text and graphics to appear on-screen as you want. When you save the document as an HTML file, Word converts the formatting in the document to the HTML codes required to reproduce the same or a similar appearance. However, not all Word formatting can be converted to HTML codes. This means that the final HTML document might not look exactly like the original Word document.

One difference between Web pages and regular Word documents is that a Web page can have a title, which is displayed in the browser's title bar when the page is viewed on the Web. Word allows you to assign a title to a document saved as a Web page.

Use the following steps to save a Word document as an HTML file:

1. Select **File, Save as Web Page** to open the Save As dialog box. The Save as Type box automatically specifies Web Page as the document type.

2. Enter the filename in the **File Name** text box.

3. Click the **Change Title** button to display the Set Page Title dialog box.

4. Enter or edit the page title, then click **OK** to return to the Save As dialog box.

5. Click **OK**.

  Quick Web Pages   When you are editing a Web page, the New Blank Document button on the Standard toolbar changes to the New Web Page button; you can click this button to create a new, blank Web page.

EDITING A WEB DOCUMENT

You can use Word to edit existing Web documents in HTML format. When you open an HTML document, it is converted into Word format. When you save it, the document is converted back to HTML format. Use the following steps to open an HTML document for editing:

1. Select **File, Open** or click the **Open** button on the Standard toolbar to display the Open dialog box.

2. The dialog box displays all types of Word files: documents, Web pages, and templates. To limit the display to Web pages, click the **Files of Type** drop-down arrow and select **Web Pages** from the list.

3. Select the desired file in the **Files** list. (Change to a different folder first if necessary.)

4. Select **OK**. The document is displayed for editing. Word automatically switches to Web Layout view when you open a Web document.

5. Use Word's regular editing commands to make changes to the document.

6. Select **File, Save** or click the **Save** button on the Standard toolbar. The document is automatically saved in HTML format.

WORKING WITH LINKS

A *link* serves as an address or points to something on the Web, such as a Web page or a person's email address. Following are the two types of links you will encounter most often:

- A mail-to link specifying an individual's email address; for example, `jsmith@abc.com`.

- A hypertext link identifying a Web document; for example, `http://www.abc.com`.

Word has the capability to recognize links in a document and to treat them as links rather than as plain text. Links differ from plain text as follows:

- The link is displayed in a special color or is underlined, or both.

- When you point at the link with your mouse, the mouse pointer changes to a pointing hand.

- When you click a hypertext link, a new Word window opens and displays the Web page that the link points to—but only if you are connected to the Internet.

- When you click a mail-to link, your email program automatically starts and displays a blank message already addressed to the link address.

The automatic activation of your Web browser and email program is, of course, dependent on these programs being installed on your system. By doing the following, you can have Word automatically detect text that represents links as you type:

1. Select **Tools, AutoCorrect** to open the AutoCorrect dialog box.

2. If necessary, click the **AutoFormat As You Type** tab.

3. Select the **Internet and Network Paths With Hyperlinks** check box.

4. Select **OK**.

Another approach is to have Word go through existing text, locating link text and converting it. Following are the steps required to convert links:

1. Select **Format, AutoFormat** to open the AutoFormat dialog box.

2. Select the **AutoFormat Now** check box.

3. Click the **Options** button to display the AutoFormat tab of the AutoCorrect dialog box, as shown in Figure 25.1.

4. Select the **Internet and Network Paths with Hyperlinks** check box.

5. Deselect all the other check boxes.

6. Select **OK** to return to the AutoFormat dialog box.

7. Click **OK**.

Use the following steps to convert a link back to regular text:

1. Right-click the hyperlink to display the pop-up menu.

2. Select **Hyperlink, Remove Hyperlink** from the submenu.

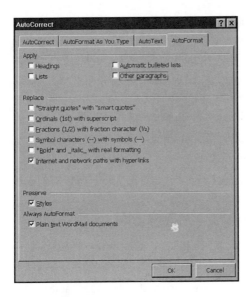

FIGURE 25.1   Setting AutoFormat options to automatically format hyperlinks.

INSERTING A LINK

If you're working on a document, you can insert a link by simply typing its address and allowing Word to automatically identify it (as previously described). An easier way is to use the **Insert Hyperlink** command. You can link to Internet files, Word documents, and various other types of files as follows:

1. Select the text that you want displayed as the hyperlink.

2. Select **Insert**, **Hyperlink** or press **Ctrl+K**. The Insert Hyperlink dialog box appears (see Figure 25.2).

    Quick Links   To quickly create a hyperlink, select the text, then click the **Insert Hyperlink** button on the Standard toolbar.

3. If the document or Web page that you want to link to already exists, be sure that the **Existing File or Web Page** icon is selected under the Link To heading at the left edge of the dialog box.

4. If you know the address of the document you want to link to, type it in the **Type the File or Web Page Name** text box. You can also select a link in one of the following ways:

   • Click **Recent Files** to select from documents you opened recently in Word.

   • Click **Browsed Pages** to select from Web pages that you viewed recently using your Web browser.

   • Click **File...** to browse for a file on your computer.

   • Click **Web Page...** to open your Web browser to locate a page on the Web.

5. You can also select one of the other icons at the left edge of the dialog box:

   • Select **Place in This Document** to link to a specific location in the current document.

   • Select **Create New Document** to create a new document to which the link will point.

   • Select **Email Address** to create a link to an email address.

6. Click **OK**.

Use the Web Toolbar   Word's Web toolbar provides quick access to many Internet-related commands. To display it, select View, Toolbars, Web or click the Web Toolbar button on the Standard toolbar.

EDITING A LINK

You can edit an existing hyperlink in your document as follows:

1. Right-click the link, and then select **Hyperlink** from the pop-up menu.

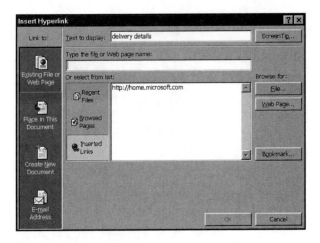

FIGURE 25.2   To Add a hyperlink to a document, use the Insert Hyperlink dialog box.

2. Select **Edit Hyperlink** from the submenu. The Edit Hyperlink dialog box is displayed; this dialog is essentially identical to the Insert Hyperlink dialog box (shown in Figure 25.2).

3. Make the required changes to the hyperlink text or URL.

4. Click **OK**.

In this lesson you learned how to use Word's Web-related features. The next lesson, "Revision Marks, Multiple Versions, and Web Collaboration," shows you how to use revision marks, multiple versions, and Web collaboration.

LESSON 26

REVISION MARKS, MULTIPLE VERSIONS, AND WEB COLLABORATION

In this lesson, you learn how to use Word's revision, version, and Web collaboration capabilities.

WHY USE REVISIONS?

Word's revision features are very useful when more than one person is working on a document. For example, an author can send a document to an editor, who then enters suggested changes to text and formatting. With revision marks, both the original text and the suggested changes are present in the document. When the document is returned to the author, he or she can review the suggested changes and either accept or reject them. When a document is reviewed by more than one person, each reviewer's suggested changes can be uniquely identified by the text color.

TRACKING AND HIGHLIGHTING DOCUMENT CHANGES

Keeping track of changes and highlighting them in the document are two independent processes. There are three ways in which this can work:

- If you track changes without highlighting them, Word keeps track of document changes but does not display revision marks on the screen. You can later turn on the revision marks to show the previous changes.

- If you highlight changes without tracking them, changes that were made to the document when tracking was turned on are highlighted, but new changes are not tracked or marked.

- If you both track and highlight changes, Word tracks new changes and marks both old and new ones. You will probably use this setting most often.

You can also control whether revision marks are included when the document is printed. To control the tracking and marking of changes in a document, use the following steps:

1. Select **Tools**, **Track Changes**, and then select **Highlight Changes**. The Highlight Changes dialog box appears (see Figure 26.1).

2. Select or deselect the **Track Changes While Editing** and the **Highlight Changes on Screen** check boxes as desired. If you also want the changes highlighted when the document is printed, select the **Highlight Changes in Printed Document** check box.

3. Select **OK**.

FIGURE 26.1 Control how revision marks work in the Highlight Changes dialog box.

Fast Track   To quickly turn tracking of document changes on or off, double-click the TRK indicator in Word's status bar. This toggles the Track Changes While Editing check box on or off.

Revision marks are displayed as follows:

- Changed text (text that is added or deleted) is displayed in a different color and with a vertical line in the outside margin; the color of the text identifies the reviewer who made the changes. If multiple individuals have revised the document, each person's revisions are displayed in a different color (with a maximum of eight reviewers).

- Newly added text is displayed with an underline, <u>like this</u>.

- Deleted text is displayed with strikethrough, ~~like this~~.

SETTING REVISION MARK OPTIONS

Word enables you to control the way that revised text is marked. Use the following steps to set these options:

1. Select **Tools, Track Changes,** and then select **Highlight Changes** to open the Highlight Changes dialog box (refer to Figure 26.1).

2. Click the **Options** button to open the Track Changes dialog box (see Figure 26.2).

3. There are four types of changes that Word can mark: inserted text, deleted text, changed formatting, and changed lines. To specify the type of mark used for each type of change, click the **Mark** drop-down arrow in the corresponding section of the dialog box and select the mark from the list. Select **(none)** if you do not want this type of change marked.

4. For each type of change, click the **Color** drop-down arrow and select the color to be used. If you select **By Author,** Word automatically assigns a different color to each of as many as eight reviewers. If you select a specific color, all changes are marked with that color—regardless of who made them.

5. Select **OK**.

Who Am I?   Word identifies document reviewers by the user information that you enter. This information is used by all Microsoft Office applications—not just Word. Select **Tools, Options,** and then click the **User Information** tab to view or change your user information.

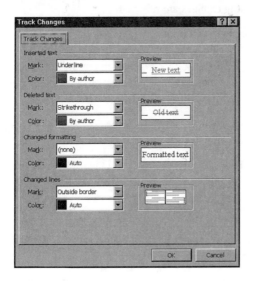

FIGURE **26.2**   Specify how Word marks document changes in the Track Changes dialog box.

ACCEPTING OR REJECTING CHANGES

After a document has been reviewed by one or more reviewers, you need to go through the text and either accept or reject the suggested changes. When you accept changes

- Text identified as Inserted is made part of the document.

- Text identified as Deleted is permanently deleted.

- Formatting changes are permanently applied.

- Revision marks are removed.

When you reject changes

- Text identified as Inserted is removed.

- Text identified as Deleted is restored.

- Formatting changes are reversed.

- Revision marks are removed.

You can accept or reject all the changes in one step or you can browse through the document, viewing individual changes and accepting or rejecting them one at a time. Here are the steps to follow:

1. Move the cursor to the place in the document at which you want to start reviewing changes.

2. Select **Tools, Track Changes,** and then select **Accept or Reject Changes.** The Accept or Reject Changes dialog box appears, as shown in Figure 26.3.

3. You can click in the document and scroll around while keeping the dialog box displayed. In the View area of the dialog box, select how you want the document displayed:

    - **Changes with Highlighting** Displays both the changes and the revision marks.

    - **Changes without Highlighting** Displays the changes but not the revision marks.

    - **Original** Hides both the changes and the revision marks.

4. Select **Accept All** or **Reject All** to accept or reject all the changes in the document.

5. To review individual changes, click ←**Find** or →**Find** to move to the previous or next change in the document. In the Changes area of the dialog box, Word highlights the change and displays information about the identity of the reviewer, the change made (for example, Inserted or Deleted), and the date and time of the

change. You can then click **Accept** or **Reject** to accept or reject
the change.

6. Repeat step 5 until you have reviewed all the revisions in the
document.

7. Click **Undo** to reverse the most recent acceptance or rejection.

8. When you are finished, select **Close**.

FIGURE 26.3   Use the Accept or Reject Changes dialog box to accept
or reject document changes.

USING DOCUMENT VERSIONS

Sometimes you might want to save different versions of a document as
you work on it. One way to do this is to select **File, Save As** to save each
version of the document under a different filename. Word also enables
you to keep different versions of a document together in a single file,
making them easier to keep track of and saving disk space.

Follow these steps to save the current document version:

1. Select **File, Versions** to open the Versions dialog box (see Figure
26.4). If any previous versions of this document were saved,
they are listed.

2. Click the **Save Now** button.

3. Enter any comments to identify the current version. The date and
time are automatically included.

4. Select **OK**.

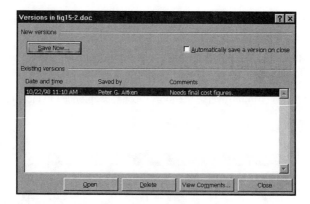

FIGURE 26.4   Use the Versions dialog box to work with different versions of a document.

 AutoVersion Select the **Automatically Save a Version on Close** check box in the Versions dialog box if you want Word to save a version of the document each time you close it.

Follow these steps to view or delete a specific version of the current document:

1. Select **File, Versions** to open the Versions dialog box (refer to Figure 26.4).

2. Select the desired version from the **Existing Versions** list, which displays all versions of the document.

3. Click **Open** to display the version, or click **Delete** to delete the version.

When you display an earlier version of a document, you can view and print it, but you cannot edit it. If you want to modify a previous version, you must first save it as a separate document by selecting **File, Save As**.

WEB COLLABORATION

Word's Web Collaboration feature enables you to share a document with your colleagues over the Internet or an intranet, and to conduct online discussions related to the document. To use this feature you must have access to an Office Server, a special type of Web server that is set up to permit Web Collaboration. Your network administrator will provide you with the address of the Office Server, which will have the same form as a regular Web address (such as http://office2000.yourcompany.com). You will also be given a user ID and a password, which are required for authorized access to the server. A password is not required in all cases.

OPENING AND SAVING DOCUMENTS ON THE WEB SERVER

To collaborate on a Web document and participate in any discussions related to it, you must open the document. Follow these steps:

1. Click on **File**, **Open** to display the Open dialog box.

2. Under Look In, click the **Web Folders** icon.

3. The dialog box lists any Web servers that are already set up. If you see the name of the server that you want to use, double-click it and go to step 7.

4. If the desired Web server is not listed, click on the **Create New Folder** button to display the Add Web Folder dialog box (Figure 26.5).

5. Enter the address of the server in the text box, and then click the **Next** button. Your computer might take a moment to verify that the server is responding.

6. In the next dialog box, enter the name that you will use to identify this server, and then click **Finish**.

7. At this point you might be asked to log on. Enter your username and password for Web server access, and then click **OK**.

8. The Open dialog box now displays a list of documents available on the Web server, as shown in Figure 26.6.

FIGURE 26.5   Use the Add Web Folder dialog box to connect to a Web Collaboration server.

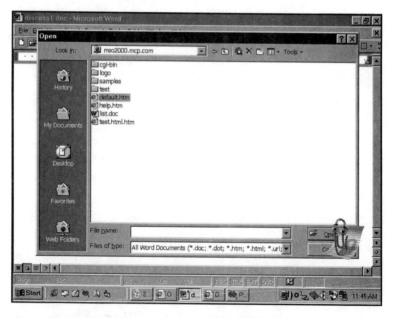

Figure 26.6   Use the Open dialog box to open a document from a Web Collaboration server.

9. Click the name of the desired document, and then click **Open** to open the document for editing.

When you open a document on a Web server, it is automatically saved back to the server when you click **File, Save**. If you have created a new document or have opened a document from your local hard disk, here's how to save the document to a Web server:

1. Click on **File, Save As** to display the Save As dialog box.

2. Under Save In, click the **Web Folders** icon. The dialog box lists the Web server(s) you have set up. If you have not yet set up a Web server, follow the steps given in the section on opening a document from a Web server to enter your server information.

3. Double-click the name of the Web server on which you want to save the document. If prompted, enter your username and password.

4. Enter the document name in the **File Name** box.

5. Click the **Save** button. Word saves the document on the Web server.

PARTICIPATING IN WEB DISCUSSIONS

When you participate in a Web discussion, you can add comments to a document and read comments that have been added by others. Other participants in the discussion can read your comments as well. You can also choose to be notified whenever anyone else modifies the document (but only if the Notification feature is set up on your server). To work with a discussion related to the current document, click on **Tools, Online Collaboration, Web Discussions**. Word displays the Discussions toolbar at the bottom of the screen, as shown in Figure 26.7. Depending on the status of your document and the discussion, some of the toolbar buttons might not be available (grayed out). Unless the document has no discussions entered yet, Word also opens the discussion pane (also shown in Figure 26.7).

There are two types of discussions that can be associated with a document. An inline discussion is used to refer to a specific part of the document, such as a paragraph or a table, whereas a *general discussion* refers to the document as a whole. Each inline discussion is represented by an icon at the document location where the discussion was added, whereas general discussions are not represented by icons in the document. Otherwise, the two types of discussions are handled in essentially the same way.

Insert Discussion In the
Document button

Insert Discussion About
the Document button

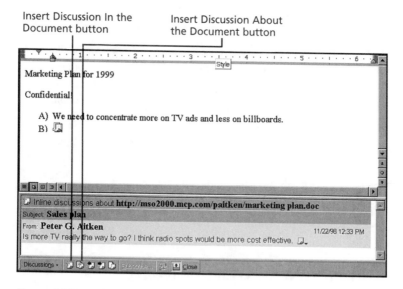

FIGURE 26.7   Using Word's discussion pane and toolbar.

Follow these steps to add a discussion to a document:

1. If you are adding an inline discussion, move the cursor to the location in the document to which the discussion refers. If you are adding a general discussion, the cursor position does not matter.

2. On the discussion toolbar, click the **Insert Discussion In the Document** button (to add an inline discussion) or click the **Insert Discussion About the Document** button (to add a general discussion).

3. Word opens the Enter Discussion Text dialog box. Enter the subject of the discussion in the **Discussion Subject** box and the text of the discussion in the **Discussion Text** box.

4. Click on **OK**. Word displays the discussion item in the discussion pane. If you entered an inline discussion, an icon is inserted in the document.

The following list explains the actions you can take while working with discussions in a document:

- To view the next or previous discussion in the document, click the **Next** or the **Previous** button on the Discussion toolbar.

- To view a specific inline discussion, click its icon in the document.

- To view general discussions, click the **Show General Discussions** button on the Discussions toolbar.

- To subscribe to a document or folder and receive email notification whenever changes are made, click the **Subscribe** button and enter your email address and other requested information. To cancel a subscription, follow the instructions in one of the notification messages you receive.

- To refresh discussions so that you can read any material that was added since you downloaded the document, click on the **Discussions** button on the Discussions toolbar, and then click on **Refresh Discussions**.

- To display only discussions from a specific participant or entered within a specified time period, click on the **Discussions** button on the Discussions toolbar, then click on **Filter Discussions** and enter the requested information in the dialog box that is displayed.

- To change which parts of a discussion (Username, Subject, Text, and Time) are displayed in the discussion pane, click on the **Discussions** button on the Discussions toolbar, click on **Discussion Options**, and then select options in the Discussion Options dialog box.

- To reply to a discussion, click the icon at the end of the text in the discussion pane and then click on **Reply**. The Enter Discussion Text dialog box is displayed with the subject already entered. Type your reply in the **Discussion** text box, and then click **OK**.

- To edit or delete a discussion, click the icon at the end of the text in the discussion pane and click on **Edit** or **Delete**. You can edit or delete only discussion items you have added, not those from other people.

- To hide the discussion pane and toolbar, click the **Close** button on the Discussions toolbar. To display them again, click **Tools, Online Collaboration, Web Discussions**.

This lesson showed you how to use Word's revision and version capabilities, how to save and open documents on a Web server, and how to participate in online discussions. In the next lesson, "Customizing the Way Word Works," you will learn how to customize Word.

Lesson 27

Customizing the Way Word Works

In this lesson you learn how to customize Word to suit your preferences.

Customizing the Toolbars

Word provides a number of toolbars, each containing buttons for commands related to certain document tasks (such as formatting or drawing). The Formatting and Standard toolbars are displayed by default, together on a single row under the menu bar. You can display each as its own row, if preferred, to permit the display of more buttons at a time. Here are the steps to follow:

1. Select **Tools, Customize** to display the Customize dialog box.

2. Click the **Options** tab (see Figure 27.1).

3. Turn off the **Standard and Formatting Toolbars Share One Row** option.

You can customize the buttons that are shown on any toolbar, adding and removing buttons to suit your own working style. The commands that can be added to a toolbar include Word's regular menu commands, as well as fonts, styles, and macros. Here are the steps to follow:

1. Be sure that the toolbar you want to customize is displayed. If it is not, select **View, Toolbars**, and then select the desired toolbar.

2. Select **Tools, Customize** to open the Customize dialog box. Click the **Commands** tab (see Figure 27.2).

FIGURE 27.1   Control how the Standard and Formatting toolbars are displayed in the Customize dialog box.

3. In the **Categories** list, select the category related to the command you want to add. If you cannot locate a specific command under a category, try selecting the **All Commands** option. Macros, fonts, styles, and AutoText entries have their own categories.

4. The Commands list displays the commands in the category you selected. The actions you can take are as follows:

   - To add a button to a toolbar, drag it from the Commands list to the desired position in the toolbar. When the pointer is over the toolbar, a vertical black line is displayed showing the position where the button will be placed.

   - To remove a button from a toolbar, drag it from the toolbar and drop it anywhere in the document.

   - To move a button from one toolbar to another, drag it from the old location to the new location.

   - To copy a button so that it is present on both toolbars, hold down **Ctrl** while dragging the button from one toolbar to another.

5. When finished, select **Close**.

Quickly Move a Button   You can quickly move a toolbar button to a different toolbar or to a new position on the same toolbar without opening the Customize dialog box. Simply hold down the Alt key and drag the button to the new location.

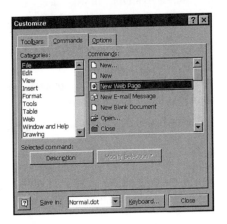

FIGURE 27.2   Use the Customize dialog box to add or remove buttons on the toolbars.

 Restoring Defaults   To return a customized toolbar to its default settings, select Tools, Customize, and click the Toolbars tab. Select the toolbar in the list and click the Reset button.

CREATING A NEW TOOLBAR

You can create completely new toolbars, arranging their command buttons to suit your personal editing needs and work habits. Use the following steps to create a toolbar:

1. Select **Tools, Customize** to open the Customize dialog box.

2. Click the **Toolbars** tab.

3. Click the **New** button. The New Toolbar dialog box appears (see Figure 27.3).

4. In the **Toolbar Name** text box, enter a descriptive name for the toolbar.

5. In the **Make Toolbar Available To** list, select where the new toolbar will be available. The options are as follows:

    • **Normal**   All documents.

    • (*Template Name*)   If the current document is based on a template other than Normal, the toolbar is available only in documents based on that template.

    • (*Document Name*)   The toolbar is available only in the current document.

6. The new toolbar will be created and displayed; it will be empty, of course. Follow the steps in the section "Customizing Toolbars" (earlier in this chapter) to add buttons to your new toolbar.

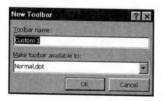

FIGURE 27.3   Use the New Toolbar dialog box to create a new toolbar.

CUSTOMIZING THE MENUS

You can customize Word's menus, adding and deleting commands as you see fit. You can also create new menus and add the commands you want to them. Here are the steps to follow:

1. Select **Tools, Customize** to open the Customize dialog box. Click the **Commands** tab (refer to Figure 27.2).

2. In the **Categories** list, select the category of the command you want to add, or select **All Commands** to list all available commands. Macros, fonts, styles, and AutoText entries have their own categories.

3. Point at the desired command in the list and drag it to the menu bar, over the name of the menu where you want to place it (do not release the mouse button yet). The menu opens. Continue dragging until the command is at the desired menu location, and then release the mouse button.

4. To create a new menu, select **New Menu** in the **Categories** list; then drag the **New Menu** command from the **Commands** list to the desired position on the menu bar. Right-click the menu title to change its name or to delete it.

5. To delete a command, click its menu open, and then drag the command off the menu.

6. When you are finished, click **Close**.

CUSTOMIZING THE KEYBOARD

When you customize the keyboard, you assign *shortcut keys* to specified commands. A shortcut key is a key or key combination that you can press to carry out the command, just as if you had selected the command from a menu or a toolbar. You can assign regular Word commands to shortcut keys, and you can also assign styles, macros, fonts, and AutoText entries.

Word comes with many commands already assigned to shortcut keys. You can change or delete these assignments, but use caution. Some shortcut keys are standardized across different Windows programs, such as Ctrl+O for Open, Ctrl+Z for Undo, and Ctrl+F for Find. If you change these assignments, you run the risk of making your copy of Word too different from other Windows programs.

Following are the steps needed to assign a shortcut key:

1. Select **Tools**, **Customize** to open the Customize dialog box.

2. Click the **Keyboard** button to open the Customize Keyboard dialog box, shown in Figure 27.4.

3. Select the desired category of command in the **Categories** list. Macros, styles, fonts, common symbols, and AutoText have their own categories at the end of the list.

4. Select the desired command in the **Commands** list. If there is currently a shortcut key assigned to the command, it appears in the Current Keys list.

5. To remove an assigned key from the command, highlight it in the **Current Keys** list and select **Remove**.

6. To add a shortcut key for the command, click the **Press New Shortcut Key** text box, then press the desired key or key combination. The key description appears in the text box. If that shortcut key is currently assigned to a command, it is indicated below the box. Otherwise, **(unassigned)** appears.

7. To assign the shortcut key (and unassign it from its previous command, if any), select **Assign**. To enter another shortcut key, press **Backspace**, then return to step 6.

8. Click the **Save Changes In** drop-down arrow and, from the list, select where the shortcut key will be saved.

9. Select **Remove** to delete the key assignment you just made. Select **Reset All** to remove all custom shortcut keys and return Word to its default key assignments.

 Make a List If you assign some custom shortcut keys, you might want to make a list of them for your own reference. You can print the list in a small font and tape it to the edge of your monitor for easy reference.

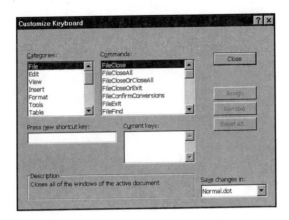

FIGURE 27.4   Using the Customize Keyboard dialog box to assign shortcut keys to commands.

This lesson showed you how to customize Word to suit your needs and work habits. This is the last lesson in the book, so I will say good-bye and wish you good luck.

INDEX

S

Save As command
(File menu), 185
Save As dialog box, 26, 185
saving documents, 25-27
    changing document
    name, 27
    HTML, 26
    multiple documents, 27, 181
    versions, 199-200
    Web documents, 203
screen
    document size, 53-54
    elements, 2-3
    splitting, 55-57
    views, 47, 51
        Draft Font view, 52
        Full Screen view, 53
        graphics, 170-171
        Normal view, 47-48
        Outline view, 51
        Print Layout view,
        48-49
        Web Layout view, 50
scroll bars, 3, 18-19
Search template, 43
searching for text, 42-45
    and replacing 45-46
selecting
    menu commands, 4
    text, 19
        keyboard, 21
        mouse, 20
sentences, selecting, 20
setting indents, 87
shading, 79, 82-83
shortcut keys, 5-6, 211-212

sizing
    documents, 53-54
    graphics, 171
    paper, 127-128
spacing, paragraphs, 115-116
special characters, 145, 149-150
    inserting, 147
spell checking, 58-60, 62-63
Spelling and Grammar
    dialog box, 60
splitting screen, 55-57
Standard toolbar, 3, 6, 18
Start menu, 1
starting
    multiple documents, 175-176
    Word, 1
status bar, 3
styles
    assiging to text, 104-105
    creating, 107-108
    customizing, 109-110
    deleting, 105
    finding, 118-120
    formatting, 103-104,
        111-112
    heading styles, 112-115
    keyboard shortcuts, 116-118
    paragraph spacing, 115-116
    replacing, 118-120
    Style list, 106
submenu arrows, 5
switching between documents,
    176-177
Symbol dialog box, 146
symbols, 145
    inserting, 145-146
    keyboard shortcuts, 147-149
syntax, spell checking, 60

word wrapping, 16
words, counting in documents,
  30
work area, 3
World Wide Web, *see* WWW
wrapping text, 16
WWW (World Wide Web)
  accessing, 187
  documents, 201
    creating, 187-188
    discussions, 203-206
    editing, 188-189
    opening, 201-203
    saving, 203
  links, 189-190
    editing, 192-193
    inserting, 191-193

Zoom dialog box, 53
zooming, 53-54